Malaysia
A Kick Start Guide for Business Travelers

Malaysia
A Kick Start Guide for Business Travelers

Guy & Victoria Brooks

Self-Counsel Press
(*a division of*)
International Self-Counsel Press Ltd.
Canada U.S.A.

Copyright © 1995 by International Self-Counsel Press Ltd.
All rights reserved.

No part of this book may be reproduced or transmitted in any form by any means — graphic, electronic, or mechanical — without permission in writing from the publisher, except by a reviewer who may quote brief passages in a review.

Printed in Canada

First edition: February, 1995

Canadian Cataloguing in Publication Data
Brooks, Guy, 1955-
    Malaysia

    (Self-counsel business series)
    ISBN 0-88908-845-4

1. Malaysia — Guidebooks. 2. Malaysia — Economic conditions. 3. Business travel — Malaysia. I. Brooks, Victoria, 1951- II. Title. III. Series.
DS591.5.B76   1995   915.9504'54   C95-910124-1

Self-Counsel Press
(*a division of*)
International Self-Counsel Press Ltd.

Head and Editorial Office	*U.S. Address*
1481 Charlotte Road	1704 N. State Street
North Vancouver, B.C.	Bellingham, Washington
V7J 1H1	98225

To our son, Tyson Brooks, who through his flexible and open attitude to life has allowed us so much traveling time together.

Contents

	Introduction	xvii
1	**Malaysia — The Land and the People**	1
	Malaysia Positives	1
	Malaysia Negatives	2
	Country Profile	3
	Area	3
	Location	3
	Divisions	4
	Population	4
	People	4
	Religion	5
	Politics	5
	Questions for the Future	8
2	**Opening the Door — and Keeping It Open**	10
	Preparation	10
	Letters of Introduction	11
	Appointments and Contacts	12
	The Etiquette of Business	13
	Communication Gaps	13

Etiquette and Understanding	14
Being on Time	15
Using Names and Titles	15
Hierarchy and Status	16
Business Cards and Greetings	17
Body Etiquette	17
Social Taboos	18
The Correct Attitude	19
Negotiations	20
3 Basics for the business traveler	**21**
Language	21
Climate	22
What to Wear	23
Visas	24
Health Matters	25
What to Bring	26
Business Hours	28
Currency and Credit Cards	28
Exchanging Your Money	29
Tipping	29
Bargaining	30
Making Phone Calls	30
Telephone Area Codes	31
Electricity	32
Time Zones	32
Holidays	32

Contents

	News Media	33
	English-Language Papers	34
	Airlines	35
4	**An Expedient Arrival in Kuala Lumpur**	37
	Planning Your Arrival	37
	Arrival Forms	37
	Arrival	38
	Getting to the Hotel	40
5	**Highlights of the Major Cities**	42
	Kuala Lumpur	42
	The Importance of Kuala Lumpur	44
	City Patterns	44
	Kota Kinabalu	48
	Kuching	51
	Malaysia's Ports	53
6	**Getting Around with Ease**	54
	Taxis	54
	Buses	55
	Car Rentals	56
	Driving in Malaysia	58
	Trains	60
	Ferry Service	61
	Airline Travel	61

Malaysia: A Kick Start Guide

7	**An Economic Overview for Business**	63
	Economic Growth	64
	Sixth Malaysia Plan	64
	Vision 2020	65
	MASSA	66
	Tariffs	67
	Inflation	68
	Average Income	69
	Currency	69
	Employment	70
	Infrastructure	70
	Consumerism	72
	Manufacturing	74
	Mining	76
	Oil and Gas	77
	Agriculture	78
8	**Special Economic Zones**	79
	Free Trade Zones	79
	Industrial Estates	80
	Selangor	81
	Penang	81
	Perak	82
	Johor	83
	Labuan for Entrepreneurs	84

Contents

9	**Joint Ventures and Doing Your Business**	89
	Malaysian Investment Development Agency (MIDA)	90
	Non-Resident Controlled Company (NRCC)	91
	Joint Venture Rules	91
	The Local Partner	93
	Privatization	94
	Income Tax	94
	Company Tax	95
	Tax Incentives	96
	Pioneer Status	96
	Investment Tax Allowance	96
	Export Incentives — Double Deductions	97
	Double Taxation	97
10	**Banks, Investments, and Financial Services Opportunities**	99
	Banking	99
	Foreign Banks	99
	The Central Bank	101
	Local Banks	101
	Securities Market	103
	Education	104
	Employers Provident Fund	105
	Foreign Exchange	108
	Mutual Funds	108

Malaysia: A Kick Start Guide

11	**Best Buys: Sabah and Sarawak**	112
	Around Kuala Lumpur	112
	Silk	112
	Pewter	112
	Kelantan State	113
	Silverware	113
	Songket	113
	Batik	114
	Traditional Woodcarvings, Kites, and Tops	114
	Sarawak	114
	Woven Straw and Bamboo	114
	Beadwork	115
	Pottery	115
	Primitive Art	115
	Shipping	116
12	**Where to Stay**	117
	Hotel Listings	118
	Kuala Lumpur and Area	119
	Apartments (For longer stays or with family)	124
	Airport Hotels	124
	Kuching Sarawak	125
	Kota Kinabalu, Sabah	126
	Golfing Getaways	126

Beach Getaways	127
Pangor Islands	127
Langkawi	128
Island of Borneo	129
Sarawak	129
Sabah	131

Maps

Malaysia	xvi
Kuala Lumpur	46
Kota Kinabalu	49
Kuching	52

Notice to Readers

Every effort is made to keep this publication as current as possible. However, it is the nature of travel books that some information could become outdated between the time of writing and publication. Prices, telephone and fax numbers, addresses, and hours of operations of businesses are subject to change without notice. Readers are asked to take this into account when consulting this guide.

The authors, the publisher, and the vendor of this book make no representation or warranties regarding the outcome or the use to which the information in this book is put and are not assuming any liability for any claims, losses, or damages arising out of the use of this book. The reader should not rely on the authors or the publisher of this book for any professional advice.

Introduction

Who Should Read *Malaysia*

This guide was specifically researched and written for the business traveler who has little practical knowledge of Malaysia. It is also for the entrepreneur, always on the lookout for new opportunities in Malaysia's high-performing economy. New opportunities abound, especially in manufacturing, exporting, service, and in consumer, corporate, and financial services.

Take these facts into consideration:

- Malaysia is one of the world's most rapidly developing countries. The stock market is booming, real estate and construction is at a record high, and manufacturing and economic growth is set to stay at more than 6% to 7% a year into the next century.
- In the last two decades, the poverty rate has dropped dramatically from 49.3% to 13.5%. Malaysians are "consumer hot."
- The Malaysian government is now trying to attract M $33 billion of overseas investment for the manufacturing sector. Approved overseas investment between 1980 and the mid-1990s

topped the M $56 billion mark. This means great opportunities in infrastructure facilities, manufacturing, and service industries, such as banking, hotels, etc.
- In the 21st century, the Asia Pacific economy will be even stronger than NAFTA's.

Yes, Malaysia is hot for foreign investment and business opportunities, especially in the domestic market. There is a growing demand among Malaysians for consumer products. To meet the demand, the government wants to expand the manufacturing base and build on the existing infrastructure. There are opportunities to sell your skills and products to the ever-growing corporate, mining, construction, agriculture, and service sector, strategic alliances of all kinds, and export-oriented manufacturing. Further, Malaysia's government is pro-business and liberal on foreign investment. Malaysia's labor force is competitive in the Asian market and is, generally speaking, becoming increasingly skilled and reliable. Added to all this is the wonderful fact that most Malaysians speak English.

If any of this makes you smile, Malaysia might be for you. Increasingly, foreign entrepreneurs are recognizing and taking advantage of Malaysia's already-existing infrastructure and looking for new opportunities.

But to do business in Malaysia you need to adapt to a different culture. Time, persistence, and patience are the keys to business success in Malaysia. Many entrepreneurs, in too much of a hurry, have lost out to other individuals or companies who had more time, endurance, and stamina. Business in Malaysia requires a long-term commitment. If you come armed with the right knowledge of how to do business, the rewards are well worth the effort.

How To Use *Malaysia*

Our task in writing this guide was to show you, the interested business traveler, how to begin the research and groundwork necessary to do business in Malaysia while avoiding common but usually unknown pitfalls. This book tells you what you need to know to make your trip comfortable and interesting. We also sincerely hope it will give you an appreciation of the country and help you answer the question: Do you really want to do business or spend time there?

Malaysia outlines in a concise, interesting, and often personal manner, the cultural idiosyncrasies that you need to know to be effective in business. The result will be an easier adjustment for you, which means your mind can focus on business matters, not on overcoming culture shock!

The groundwork and information will be of general interest to anyone on a first-time business mission to Malaysia. You will learn where to get the best rate of exchange, how to leave the airport in the most expedient manner, and the best means of getting around. Just as important, the book shows you how to quickly and comfortably set up the all-important initial visit.

Entrepreneurial tips provide suggestions on many sectors of business, including manufacturing, securities, investment, and a special section on financial services. A few interesting art and craft buying opportunities have also been noted. Malaysia has great golf holidays and beautiful tropical island retreats, and we've mentioned many of these so your trip can be coupled with a weekend retreat or a relaxing vacation.

We've also included special notes of interest: anecdotes or issues designed to help you appreciate what goes on in this country. Skip them if your time is limited!

We've done your walking for you, so you can kick start yourself into action as soon as you land.

How This Book Came About

We wrote this book together, with much help both in the research and writing from our son, Tyson, while doing a business fact-finding mission in Malaysia. We immediately saw the need for a guide like this while we were doing research for the trip. The only books available were travel guides, culture shock books, and business books that used too many statistics and graphs and had little to do with getting business done. They were useful for compiling statistics and getting addresses, but did nothing to help prepare for getting an appointment with managing

Introduction

directors, making sure you used the correct business etiquette, or getting the best value for your money.

Malaysia does not and is not meant to replace specific business books that use statistics and lists, for example, *Information Malaysia*, or *FMM Manufacturing Directory*. *Malaysia* is a supplement that gives the practical information a businessperson needs in order to be prepared and to get through the first days of a business trip without having a mini-breakdown.

1 Malaysia — the Land and the People

The picture of Malaysia as a tropical economy, solely dependent on rubber, tin, and agriculture, is the Malaysia of more than 25 years ago. When Malaysia fell into deep recession in the mid-1980s, its parliamentary-style government liberalized foreign investment. Since then it has become a roaring Asian tiger, with one of the world's most quickly developing economies.

Malaysia Positives

Malaysia's growing population of over 19 million people is becoming increasingly affluent. Malaysians are fast becoming a nation of consumers. The busy streets of Kuala Lumpur are filled with businesspeople. They stop at McDonald's, A & W, or the French baguette outlet for a quick fix of international fast food.

New office towers and condos are scraping the sky, with real estate prices recording good growth. The manufacturing sector is the rising star in Malaysia; it is set to grow more than 10% a year through the

21st century. Already over half of Malaysia's export earnings are from manufactured goods.

But it doesn't end there. The Malaysian government's sixth five-year economic plan, which ended in 1995, diversified industry, improved an already well-developed infrastructure, promoted human resource development, and upgraded technology. Economic and social stability is another plus.

> **Note of interest:** In 1993, sales of Malaysia's domestically built car, the Proton, increased 15.4%. Now, the Proton, with its logo of a crescent moon and star from Malaysia's flag, is being exported to other countries.

> **Tip:** The relatively undeveloped east coast is still available for utility and land resources.

Malaysia Negatives

Malaysia is renowned for being a tough market to crack, but it is also renowned for paying excellent rewards to patient and persistent businesspeople. It is an increasingly crowded market, where long-term involvement is the only ticket to success. The cost of doing business is increasing, but Malaysia is still competitive with other well-established countries, such as Singapore.

Foreign businesspeople say the most frustrating part of doing business in Malaysia is the cumbersome Malaysian bureaucracy and figuring out who really makes the decisions. Too many agencies and committees contribute to this problem, along with Malaysia's multi-ethnic nature and the coalition system of government. Malaysians argue there is a reason for the lengthy time span necessary to do business in Malaysia: it tests the foreign businessperson's commitment and shows good intent. Small entrepreneurs often have the upper hand over multi-national corporate executives because of less red tape and fewer time constraints.

Country Profile

Area

Malaysia's land area is 330,000 square km (127,413 square mi.) divided into two distinct areas. Peninsular or West Malaysia takes 132,000 square km (50,965 square mi.). East Malaysia, comprised of Sabah and Sarawak on the island of Borneo, takes the lion's share of 198,000 square km (76,448 square mi.).

Location

Malaysia is located in the central part of Southeast Asia. Peninsular Malaysia lies underneath Thailand and is bordered by the South China Sea on the east. It is separated from Indonesia on the west by the

Straits of Malacca. The island of Singapore lies very close off its southern tip.

East Malaysia (Sabah and Sarawak) lies on the large island of Borneo and is separated from Peninsular Malaysia by 550 km (342 mi.) of the South China Sea. Brunei borders on the north, and Indonesian Kalimantan borders it to the south.

Divisions

Malaysia is divided into 13 states, two of which are on the island of Borneo. Nine are Malay: Perlis, Kedah, Perak, Selangor, Negeri Sembilan, Johor, Pahang, Kelantan, and Terengganu. Four are non-Malay: Malacca, Penang, Sabah, and Sarawak.

The capital city, Kuala Lumpur (located in federal territory), is in the state of Selangor.

Population

Population is estimated at 18 million. The majority (approximately 82%) live in Peninsular or West Malaysia. Population growth is projected at 2.4% per year.

People

Malaysia is a multi-racial country. Approximately 62% are *Bumiputra* (i.e., those indigenous to the country: Malays, Malay-related, and aboriginal). The majority of them live in Peninsular Malaysia. In Sabah and Sarawak (East Malaysia), Malays are a minority.

Approximately 28% of the population is Chinese, and 10% are Indians and other nationalities.

> **Note of interest:** Bumiputra means "sons of the soil." Traditionally, Bumiputra had been employed in public service, but since the New Economic Policy was implemented, many have ventured into private business.

Religion

The state religion of Malaysia is Islam, and Muslims comprise the majority of the population. Malays are usually Muslim. The assimilation of ethnic groups in Malaysia is attributed to the common religion of Islam.

Freedom of worship is guaranteed by the Malaysian Constitution, and Christianity, Hinduism, and Buddhism are the other main religious groups.

In East Malaysia, the indigenous people are Christian and Animist, and the Chinese are usually Buddhist, with some Confucian and Taoist. Indians are generally Hindus; some are Muslim or Christian. Many people believe simultaneously in all of these religions.

Politics

The British came to the Straits Settlements and the Malay Peninsula in the late eighteenth century and ruled until Malaya became an independent nation in 1957, leaving its British masters behind. The Japanese invasion of the Malay States from 1941 to 1945 is said to have begun the wave of nationalism that culminated in present day Malaysia.

In 1963, the Federation of Malaysia was formed. The beginning of independence was difficult and violent, mostly due to the Chinese Malayan Communist Party struggle against the government and racial frictions.

> **Note of interest:** Islamic law dictates both religious rituals and a code of personal and social behavior. The religious rituals are belief in Allah, prayer five times a day, fasting during the month of Ramadan, giving alms, and making a pilgrimage to Mecca. If a Muslim man can afford it, he can have four wives. A man can divorce his wife by saying, "I divorce thee," three times. But a wife that has given her husband a son can only be divorced if she has given the husband legally specified cause.

Malaysia's government is a parliamentary democracy based on universal suffrage. There are 13 states plus the two federal territories of Kuala Lumpur and Labuan. Nine of these states have hereditary rulers.

The Supreme Head of State is the King (*Yang di-Pertuan Agong*) who is elected every five years from the Conference of Rulers. The government and cabinet head is the prime minister, who must be a member of the House of Representatives (*Dewan Rakyat*).

> **Note of interest:** Singapore had joined the Federation when it was established in 1963 and withdrew in 1965 to become a republic.

There are two houses of government: the fully elected Dewan Rakyat and the Senate, *Dewan Negara*, which is nominated by the King. Senate members are citizens who have given distinguished public service, have distinguished professional careers, or who represent aboriginal and racial minorities.

The supreme law is a written federal constitution. It can only be amended by a two-thirds majority in parliament. Acts passed by the Senate and the House of Representatives have to have royal approval before becoming law.

General elections are held at no more than five-year periods. The majority party is the Barisan Nasional.

Each of the 13 states handles matters that are not dealt with by the federal government through their own constitution and assembly. The non-Malay states of Sabah, Sarawak, Penang, and Malacca have an elected governor who is appointed for a four-year term by the King.

Malaysia's judiciary system is independent with power vested in the High Court of Malaysia and the High Court of Borneo. The courts are headed by Chief

Justices, with the Federal Court having exclusive jurisdiction to determine appeals. The Lord President is Head of the Judiciary.

Currently, the Barisan Nasional (National Front) is the multi-racial governing coalition. The United Malay National Organization (UMNO) is the largest party. It has headed the coalition government since independence in 1957.

The other main parties are the Malaysian Chinese Association (MCA), the Malaysian Indian Congress (MIC), and the Gerakan Party. Sarawak's leading party is called the Party Pesaka Bumiputra Bersatu (PBB).

The prime minister and head of UMNO is Datuk Seri Dr. Mahathir. Dr. Mahathir is Malaysia's fourth elected prime minister and has been the National Front leader since 1981. In 1986, he led the National Front to election victory, taking 57.4% of the vote and 148 of the 177 parliament seats. The party kept power in all of Peninsular Malaysia's legislative assemblies.

Questions for the Future

Prime Minister Mahathir bin Mohammad has won a reputation for controversy because of his rejection of western liberal values. In 1993, he boycotted the Seattle summit of Asian leaders, and he has successfully opposed western moves to link cheap labor, an obvious attraction to doing business in developing countries, with human rights.

This attitude that Asia doesn't have to kowtow to the west hasn't affected him in his own country, but the Malaysian leader's outspoken rejection of western liberal values may turn some businesspeople off.

> **Note of interest:** In 1994, in response to a London newspaper's allegations of corruption in high places in Kuala Lumpur, British companies were cut off from lucrative Malaysian government contracts.

2 Opening the Door — and Keeping It Open

Preparation

If this is your first trip to confirm the market size and potential, you should have contacts in a local law firm and an accounting firm. Your lawyer and accountant at home may have offices or affiliate offices in Kuala Lumpur, so check first. If not, your lawyer may be able to find a firm for you and give you an introduction. Time is money, but as long as you have an introduction, you are not usually charged for a first-time consultation.

If you have no contacts in Malaysia, locate firms in your home city that may have associates or even names of firms in Kuala Lumpur. Embassies, trade commissions, and associations connected with your industry will also be happy to refer you and give you contacts.

Business in Malaysia is done face-to-face — personal contact is vital — so don't be disappointed if your initial letters and faxes are not answered. A personal phone call and later a visit will ensure the beginnings of a relationship.

> **Tip:** MIDA (Malaysian Industrial Development Agency), the government body that invites foreign business to Malaysia, is highly respected and will give you introductions. MIDA has offices throughout the Asia Pacific Region, Europe, and North America. In Canada, Enterprise Malaysia helps identify opportunities, acts as a liaison for government and private sector contacts, and is very knowledgeable and helpful. The Malaysian Consulate will put you in touch with this group or a body like it.

Letters of Introduction

You will want to obtain a letter of introduction, which you can either bring with you or have your local law or accounting firm fax to its Malaysian contact. If the letter is faxed for you, be sure your objective and arrival date are clearly stated.

The local Malaysian firms receive many such requests and are happy to spend an hour or so discussing the local scene. Of course, they hope you will actually commence your project and use them to represent you.

> **Tip:** Malays love titles. If you have a title, such as President of Bigge Corp., Director of Marketing, or any designation, don't forget to put it in your letter of introduction.

Appointments and Contacts

If your time is short or you believe your contact to be very busy, it is advisable to fax ahead and confirm when you will be telephoning to make an appointment. Suggest two possible dates to ensure you get an appointment.

Don't forget to refer in your fax to your local contact or attach a letter of introduction from your contact.

You may prefer to visit your Malaysian contact *after* you have familiarized yourself with local conditions, including market appraisal. You will then be educated enough to maximize your visit.

> **Tip:** Get further relevant referrals from each appointment. Malaysians love to network and welcome friends of friends or even acquaintances. Obviously if they think they'll get some business, they will also welcome you with open arms.

The Etiquette of Business

It is of utmost importance in business and social occasions to respect, follow, and be aware of tradition, religion, and customs with the Malays.

On the whole, Malaysians are wonderful people. The typical Malaysian is warm, well-educated, honest, and easy to please. Since Malaysia's multi-racial population has lived side by side for a long time, some common traits are held by the major ethnic groups, although this does not mean that racial religious differences do not affect business.

> **Note of interest:** Malaysia devotes one-fifth of all its public spending to education. The literacy rate is 80% and education is free. However, there are not enough universities for this growing population.

Communication Gaps

A Malaysian will often choose to agree when having absolutely no intention of doing so. If a Malaysian remains silent, do not take the silence as a sign of agreement.

Many first-time business travelers from the west go home excited about the potential and think a particular deal is closer to completion than it is. Verbally confirm your discussions and negotiations as well as the other party's understanding of what you are discussing. Be simple, but not simplistic: don't patronize. If possible, get a second confirmation from the same company.

Since trust has such a high value for Bumiputras, oral agreements are usually preferred over written contracts, although in complicated business deals a simple written agreement is valued.

Like most people, Malaysians don't like criticism. Be very careful not to make your business contacts think they are losing face. This could cost you the deal!

Etiquette and Understanding

Malaysians value self-control and harmony above all else. They hide their negative feelings and are always mild mannered and polite. Their need to please makes them agree to things they have no intention of upholding. Watch out and beware!

Being on time

Malaysians are often late. The concept of time is more flexible in their minds, so often you will find them about a half-hour late for appointments. This does not mean they will accept the same from you. You must be on time.

Malaysians in the private sector tend to respect time more than their government counterparts.

> **Note of interest:** A Malaysian we know told us how he was invited to a Hilton hotel for a business meeting by some Americans. When he arrived, they were in the coffee shop tucking into the buffet lunch. The Americans didn't realize it was Ramadan, the time for fasting. Our poor Malaysian friend, not wanting to hurt their feelings, didn't say anything but endured the sight and smell of food. He hadn't eaten since midnight and couldn't concentrate on what was going on. He was also miffed that they hadn't recognized this important religious time.

Using Names and Titles
- A married woman must be addressed as *Puan*. An unmarried woman should be addressed as *Cik* (e.g., Miss Kira Friesen would be *Cik Kira*). If you are not sure if a woman is married or not, it is acceptable and polite to use the prefix Puan.
- A Malay has no surname, but add their father's names to their given names (e.g., Anwar Ibrahim should be addressed as *Encil* (Mr.) Anwar).

Titles are given by Malaysian royalty to important community members. So naturally, Malaysians are impressed by titles.

- The highest title of honor is *Tun (male)* and *Toh Puan* (his wife).
- *Datuk* or *Dato (male)* and *Datin* (his wife) is a common, less high-ranking title.
- *Tan Sri* (male) and *Puan Sri* (his wife) are chivalrous titles.
- *Tuanku* is a Malay Sultan. His children and grandchildren are *Tengku* or *Tunku*.

Note that the husband of a titled wife receives no gratuitous title, but wives do when their husband is titled.

Tip: Make sure you use titles unless you are specifically asked not to.

Hierarchy and Status

As in most Asian cultures, status, age, and position is important in Malaysia. The Malays love pomp and ceremony. Opulent offices, chauffeur-driven cars, entertainment, and business lunches are part of the status show. There is no jealousy, only a positive acceptance.

A foreigner is initially looked upon as being of lower hierarchy, and Malaysians prefer to have a proper introduction. After the introduction, a Malaysian will want to get to know you. This is the traditional way to establish trust and respect. It means little except that as a foreigner you will have to take on the Malaysian qualities of patience. Remember, everything takes a little longer.

Business Cards and Greetings

- Make sure your business card presents you in the highest possible position.
- Always present your business card at the time of introduction. Use the right hand or both hands. Do not present the card with your left hand alone. It is bad manners, as the left hand is used for personal hygiene.
- On meeting, Malay men greet each other with a simple palm to palm touch (the Malay handshake), then bring the left hand to the heart (*salaam*). The salaam signifies your handshake was sincerely accepted. (The Malay handshake is gentle by western standards.)
- The handshake used to be reserved for men only. Now, in modern urban cities like Kuala Lumpur, a man is allowed to shake a woman's hand. In rural Malaysia and in older, more conservative households, men greet women with a simple smile and a nod. Women visitors are allowed to offer their hands to both sexes.
- Kissing as a greeting is not acceptable.

Body Etiquette

- Do not kiss anyone, except for a child. Public displays of affection are not acceptable.
- The left hand alone should never be used.
- Do not point your foot at anyone. This is an insult.

- Pointing with the left hand or either index finger is also in bad form. Gesture with your right hand, palm closed, thumb up.
- Never touch anyone on the head, including children, as the head is the spiritual center of the body.
- Do not cross your legs at the knees. It is rude anytime, and it is forbidden in front of Malay royalty.
- Loud, boisterous behavior, arguing, and showing public affection to the opposite sex is distasteful.
- Aggressive behavior, including standing with hands on hips or folded in front of you, denotes a bad personality.
- Malaysians, including businessmen, value politeness and a calm, harmonious exterior above all else.

Tip: "Don't wear improper clothing, touch a head, use your left hand, or your business is dead!"

Social Taboos

- Never keep your shoes on when entering the house of a Malay or Indian.
- Men are not allowed to enter a household where their are no men at home. Women may visit women at home when no men are present, but it would be considered in poor taste if a woman

were to visit a man in his home if there were no other women present.
- Don't order pork while eating with a Muslim. It is offensive.

Tip: *Halal* means the meat was butchered in the Islamic way.

- Liquor is forbidden, although Muslims are relatively willing to accept foreigners having a drink.
- Muslims don't allow dogs in the house. It is *haram* (forbidden.)
- Chinese people prefer to eat in Chinese restaurants.
- Those who follow the Hindu religion can't eat beef.

The Correct Attitude

Bumiputras (Malays) value trust and prefer to begin business arrangements with personal, relaxed conversations to see what type of person they are dealing with. There is no hurry and these social niceties must be adhered to. *Guanxi* (a Chinese word that means "the establishment of a relationship") is important, and compromise, not aggression, is the key to successful business relationships.

Malaysians are Asians, and no Asian wants to lose face. Don't be aggressive or argumentative; you will embarrass them and put yourself in a bad light.

> **Tip:** We can't emphasize enough how important contacts are to Bumiputra. Proper introductions are the key to success.

Negotiations

- Informality, patience, and trust are essential. Formality can sometimes be mistaken for an "I am better than you" attitude.
- Malaysians appreciate a good sense of humor.
- Many deals are done over food, at lunch, or dinner.
- Although bribes are against the law, gifts for favors are accepted and appreciated.
- Communications should be to the point, with no time wasted on frivolous matters.

3 Basics for the Business Traveler

Language

The national language is Malay (Bahasa Malaysian). English is compulsory in school, and most Malaysians can both read and write in Bahasa Malaysian, English, and sometimes a third and fourth language. In almost all cases, the businessperson can get by with English.

In government business Bahasa Malaysian is used, but English translation usually follows. Remote areas are the only places where you are likely to hear Bahasa Malaysian spoken as the primary language.

> **Tip:** Although English is widely used in commerce and industry, interpreters can be found if needed in hotels, the classified section of the newspaper, and in telephone directories.

Since there is a large Chinese population, Chinese languages are spoken and Mandarin and Tamil are taught in schools. Arabic and Portuguese are also used.

Climate

The climate is tropical and sunny, with heavy rain during monsoon seasons. The average temperature is 23°C to 32°C (73°F to 90°F). The average humidity is 81%.

Kuala Lumpur is always hot. Cooler climates can be found in the hill resorts of Genting Highlands, Frasers Hill, Cameron Highlands, and Kinabalu National Park where you can enjoy a respite from the heat or a golf game. There, evening temperatures drop to around 16°C (61°F), so pack or buy a sweater.

The monsoon comes at different times to different areas. The west coast of Peninsular Malaysia has heavy downpours from May to September. Showers are not usually problematic because this part of the peninsula is sheltered by Sumatra.

The east coast of Peninsular Malaysia, Sabah, and Sarawak have the heavy rain from November to April.

Tip: Flooding during monsoon season is only a problem in rural, usually east coast areas.

What to Wear

- Men: For business, wear lightweight pants and shirt, plus tie. Short-sleeved business shirts are acceptable and help beat the ever-pervasive heat and humidity.
- Women: For business, wear informal light weight business suits, dresses with sleeves, or pants and blouses with sleeves. Women must not wear shorts or sleeveless tops. And although it is hot, pantyhose or stockings should be worn.
- Women must not wear sleeveless tops or shorts. This offends the Muslims and will earn you the wrong kind of stares. Modesty for women is important.
- Informality is fine. Malaysian batik long-sleeved shirts go from business to the fanciest social occasions with aplomb.
- At weddings, don't dress completely in black, navy, or white. Break it up with a different color. These colors are considered bad luck.
- Don't wear yellow at royal functions or at the palace. Yellow is the color that royalty wears.
- Bring sports clothes as needed: a sweater if you plan to visit the hill resorts, maybe something for a golf game.
- Umbrellas are available from your hotel concierge.

> **Tip:** Anything you need can be bought in Kuala Lumpur.

Visas

Your passport or internationally valid travel document has to be valid for a minimum of six months after your day of entry.

> **Tip:** If your country has no Malaysian representation, get your visa through the nearest Malaysian overseas mission. Business visit passes can be obtained by applying to the Malaysian Immigration Department if you need to stay longer. Again, the Malaysian Industrial Development Authority (MIDA) can help. MIDA has offices throughout the Asia Pacific region, in Europe, and in North America.

- Indian nationals must obtain a visa.
- Citizens of Israel, South Africa, and Communist countries need visas.
- No visas are necessary for British protected persons and Commonwealth citizens (except India).
- Americans and West Europeans can stay for up to three months without visas (social, business, and academic purposes only).

- Citizens of countries that have a diplomatic relationship with Malaysia don't need visas for stays up to 14 days.
- Citizens of ASEAN member states don't need visas for stays not exceeding one month.

Note: These entry regulations are subject to changes; check before you go.

Health Matters

In Kuala Lumpur, they say you can drink the tap water, but we advise you to use boiled or bottled water. In the countryside, you must make sure your water is safe. Drink only boiled or bottled water and make sure ice is made from the same. Bottled water of good quality is available everywhere.

No particular health documents are required for travel to Malaysia, but local foreign doctors recommend you be inoculated against typhoid, tetanus, diphtheria, hepatitis A, and polio. Bring anti-malaria pills to use if you plan to travel outside major cities. Check with your local hospital's travel clinic for any new recommendations before you leave.

Bring any medication you may need. Although most prescription medicines are available over the counter, they are often called by different names. If you do need to buy any type of medication, go to a decent pharmacy (apotik). On the black market you have no way of knowing the content and quality of medication. Some people stock up on medicine in Asia because some types can be quite cheap. Most types of pills are counted out individually and are priced per unit.

Note: In Malaysia, illegal drug trafficking is punishable by death. Make sure any large amounts of prescription drugs you bring into the country have their prescription labels on them. This will ensure your time is not wasted if you or your luggage happen to be searched.

If you get any sort of cut or scrape, make sure antiseptic cream is applied. Germs breed faster in the humid heat than they would elsewhere. Infections often come on quickly, even in the big cities.

Private health clinics are in all cities and the standard of facilities is very good. Many are open 24 hours. In the countryside it is easy to find good physicians who speak enough English for you to get by. Be sure to check your medical insurance to make sure that you are covered in other countries. If you aren't, buy medical travel insurance.

> **Tip:** Malaysia is excellent value for contact lenses and prescription glasses. Prices are usually lower than the country of origin.

What to Bring

If you forget some of your essentials, rest assured that most things can be bought cheaply in Kuala Lumpur. But here are a few suggestions to help make things easier.

- Don't forget your corporate brochures.
- A subscription to an out-of-country telephone calling card will help you keep your hotel telephone bill down.
- Bug repellent is important, since malaria can be rampant in the country. We found Cutter's Non-Scented to be the best. Malaria mosquitoes don't come out until around 5:00 p.m. Mosquito nets and the constant breeze of a fan will help keep mosquitoes off at night in the country.
- If you are going off the beaten track, make sure you take hypodermic syringes. If you are unfortunate enough to need an injection, you will at least be assured that the needle has not been used before.
- Bring toilet paper. You'll be fine if you get caught short in a five-star hotel or a fancy office building, but if you need to answer the call of nature in an airport or a shopping center, you may not have the luxury of toilet paper. *Tandas* indicates a public toilet. *Perempuan* means for women, and *lelaki* means for men.

Tip: Toilets are quite different in Asia. Asian-style toilets are at ground level. In most hotels and modern buildings you probably won't encounter these, but if you go anywhere else you will. Often there is one western-style toilet in one of the cubicles. Take a look before you test your thigh muscles!

Business Hours

- The weekend in large Muslim areas is Thursday afternoon and Friday.
- Businesses that do international business keep normal international hours.
- Banks are open Monday to Friday, 10:00 a.m. to 3:00 p.m., and Saturdays from 9:30 a.m. to 11:30 p.m. Banks in Kedah, Perlis, Kelantan, and Terengganu, which are Muslim states, are closed on Fridays instead of Sundays, and are open from 9:30 a.m. to 11:30 a.m. on Thursdays.
- Government hours are Monday to Thursday 8:00 a.m. to 12:45 p.m. and 2:00 p.m. to 4:15 p.m.; Fridays from 8:00 a.m. to 12.15 p.m. and 2:45 p.m. to 4:15 p.m.; Saturdays 8:00 a.m. to 12.45 p.m. The shorter hours on Friday reflect the Muslim holy day.

Currency and Credit Cards

The basic unit of currency is the ringgit, which is freely convertible. Banknotes come in M $5, M $10, M $20, M $50, M $100, M $500, and M $1,000 denominations. The ringgit is divided into 100 sen (cents). M $1 is the largest coin; these coins are commemorative issue and collectible.

Funds up to M $10,000 may be freely transferred in and out of the country. Funds above M $10,000 traveling out of the country require approval from

Basics for the Business Traveler

the Bank of Negara. Normally, approval is freely given.

Credit cards and travelers' checks are accepted in all major establishments and in the larger cities, including hotels, most restaurants, airlines, department stores, and gas stations.

> **Tip:** Keep small denominations for taxis or you'll end up leaving huge tips.

Exchanging Your Money

The best rates are available at banks, not money changers, and definitely not hotels. If you need to, you can exchange money at the automatic teller machine at the airport.

> **Tip:** Travelers' checks take a fixed handling charge, making cash better value.

Tipping

At large hotels and first class restaurants, a 10% tip is automatically added to your bill. A 5% government surcharge is also added. Consequently there is no need to tip.

Tip only on those occasions when you feel the service was really above and beyond the call of duty.

However, this does not apply to cabs and other personal services.

Bargaining

Bargaining is not expected in modern shopping centers, restaurants, hotels, department stores, and taxis. However, it is expected in markets and in the countryside.

Know what things are worth and be aware that the starting price for foreigners can be ten times or more than the real price. Keep your bargaining good natured and your purchases will be more important to you.

You can "test" the vendor by pretending you don't want the item that much and starting to walk away. If you are not called back with a final offer or the vendor doesn't accept the price you have offered, you'll either have to pay the price or go away without buying the item.

To avoid confusion when bargaining, use the word "ringgit" rather than the dollar or Malaysian dollar.

Making Phone Calls

Modern communications systems make phoning and faxing very easy, although Sabah and Sarawak are still behind the times.

Telephone cards can be purchased for calls within Malaysia. They are available at the airport, at Telecom shops, 7-Eleven stores, Petronas petrol stations, etc. Look for the signs. Uniphone and *kadfon* and some credit card phones are available in Kuala Lumpur, but they can be difficult to find. Cash phones take 10-, 20-, and 50-sen coins.

Long distance calls within Malaysia are by direct dial. International direct dial systems are in all major cities.

- For the international exchange operator, dial 108
- For direct local enquiries, dial 103
- For telegram service, dial 104
- For assisted trunk calls, dial 101

Tip: Fax and telex services are available in hotels and at marked telecommunications offices. If you encounter difficulties sending a fax, try telephoning the number first. There are quite often recorded announcements that instruct about a new number that needs to be included when dialing.

Telephone Area Codes

- Country Code — 60
- Kuala Lumpur — 3
- Penang — 4
- Johore Bahru — 7
- Perak — 5
- Kota Kinabalu, Sabah — 88

- Kuching, Sarawak — 82
- The local number usually has seven digits.

Electricity

Malaysia uses 220 volts, so bring a converter if you plan to take electrical equipment that uses 110 volts. The hotels usually have shaver converters in housekeeping.

Time Zones

Malaysian time is GMT plus eight hours. The country is 16 hours ahead of Pacific Standard Time and seven hours ahead of British Summer Time.

Holidays

As Malaysia is a multi-racial country, there are hundreds of different holidays celebrating the different regions, religions, and cultural groups. Major Christian holidays are observed throughout Malaysia. Muslim holidays, including New Year's Day, move forward by 11 days each year, due to the structure of the Muslim calendar. The 13 states also each have their own holiday.

Ramadan, a month of ritual fasting, rotates through the seasons. All Muslim adults are expected to fast from dawn to dusk. Fasting for Ramadan means business lunches are out. It also means the Muslims tend to stay up late into the night eating.

Business efficiency drops way down during this holy month. If you can schedule your business trip during the other months, do so.

- Hari Raya Haji — date varies
- Idil-Adzzha — date varies
- Idul-Fitri — date varies
- Birth of Prophet Mohammed — December 17
- Ramadan — date varies
- Chinese New Year — January or February
- Deepavali — October or November
- Labor Day — May 1
- Independence Day (Merdeka) — August 31
- Christmas — December 25
- New Year's Day — January 1
- Good Friday — April 13

Tip: Call the Malaysian Tourist Bureau or consulate to ensure businesses won't be closed during religious holidays. You can also ask the consulate which holidays will fall in the time you intend to go.

News Media

TV and radio are in Malay, Chinese, Tamil, and English.

Censorship on local news by the government is practiced and penalties are imposed.

All hotels have at least one Japanese language station, two Malaysian stations, as well as English language channels. Radio TV Malaysia has two channels (Malay and English).

English language satellite stations, including CNN World News, BBC World Service, Star TV, and a movie and entertainment channel are widely available.

> **Note of interest:** Malaysia is currently setting up its first satellite system. This move helps ensure Malaysia will keep its social and cultural integrity. Prime Minister Mahathir has been an outspoken critic of western control of Asian media.

English-Language Papers

Three English papers are published in Malaysia: *The Business Times*, *The New Straits Times*, and *The Star*.

The *International Herald Tribune, U.S.A. Today,* and other foreign English publications are available at hotels and some newsagents.

> **Tip:** *The Business Times* is the best English business paper.

Airlines

Thirty-five international airlines plus the national carrier, Malaysia Airline Systems, serve the international airport in Kuala Lumpur. Penang, Langkawi, and Kota Kinabalu also have international airports. The domestic carrier, Pelangi Air, operates throughout the Peninsula.

MAS, KLM, United, Cathay Pacific, Singapore Air, Garuda, Thai Air, and others operate daily to and from Malaysia from Asia, Europe, Australia, and the United States.

Malaysia Airlines (MAS), the national carrier, is a well-respected airline. It also has some of the cheapest fares to Malaysia available.

If you have the time, extend your trip and see more than Malaysia. It doesn't cost much more to go to a second Asian destination as long as you use the same carrier.

If you are leaving from Vancouver or Los Angeles, Cathay Pacific is a good choice, especially if you have other business in Hong Kong. If you take a holiday with your trip, check Thai Air and fly to Bangkok, then to Phuket or to the gorgeous island of Koh Samui, before or after your business trip.

KLM may be the best bet for European travelers, as it leaves from Amsterdam and other European centers.

If you can, plan to go to Bali or part of Indonesia while you are in Asia. You'll find Bali fascinating and the experience of a lifetime, one you'll never forget. Garuda is the perfect choice.

> **Tip:** MAS has some good weekend package trips to Langawi and other Malaysian beach resorts.

4 An Expedient Arrival in Kuala Lumpur

Planning Your Arrival

Malaysia is always hot. Wear the lightest clothing possible for arrival so your body doesn't get too much of a shock. A short-sleeved shirt and light pants are good enough to get you to the hotel. Women can wear anything but shorts or sleeveless tops.

> **Tip:** If you are coming from a colder climate, take lighter clothes in your carry-on baggage so that you can change on the airplane.

Arrival Forms

The flight attendants will provide you with your disembarkation card to fill in. Slip your disembarkation card into the picture page of your passport or international travel document, and keep your documents in your hand or somewhere easy to access.

Passports or travel documents are also required for travel between Peninsular Malaysia and Sabah and Sarawak. Don't forget them back in Kuala Lumpur.

You must declare any plants, fruits, soil, or insects for inspection. As well, if you've brought any video cassettes, whether for your personal entertainment in your hotel or for a business presentation, they also have to be cleared by customs. Make sure *Schindler's List* hasn't been slipped into your suitcase by mistake! (In 1994, the Malaysian government banned Spielberg's award-winning movie as "Jewish propaganda.")

Tip: Also note that North American video cassettes will not work in standard Malaysian video equipment because the technology is different. (Much of the world uses PAL technology; North America uses NTSC.) If you are relying on a tape for business purposes, talk to a technical adviser who can help you convert your tape to the different international standards — or be sure a compatible machine will be available in Malaysia.

Arrival

Subang International Airport is 24 km (15 mi.) from Kuala Lumpur.

An Expedient Arrival in Kuala Lumpur

> **Note of interest:** Malaysia's new world class airport at Sepang, southwest of Kuala Lumpur, will have a 25 million passenger capacity when opened. It will be approximately 50 km (31 mi.) from Kuala Lumpur.

After disembarking the aircraft, you must stand and wait in the immigration queuing area. Again, you'll be happier if you have changed to lighter clothes. Although the airport is modern and air-conditioned, it's still hot and muggy.

There is an ASEAN queue for member countries and queues marked for foreign passports. Look before you choose your queue. Dozens of travelers line up in the center leaving the side queues open for travelers with sharp eyes.

Follow the sign to the baggage claim area. On the wall you'll see your flight number and carrier and the baggage carousel number. There are free luggage trolleys against the wall. You'll also find porters who charge approximately U.S. $1 per bag.

After picking up your baggage, you'll line up in one of the customs lanes. Look for the green "nothing to declare" exit. This exit is for anyone who doesn't have dutiable items, but remember, if you have more than one liter of liquor, over 200 cigarettes, or gifts over M $200 (if goods are imported from Labuan, allowance for gifts jumps to M $500), you could be unlucky enough to be part of a random search and have your extra liquor confiscated.

Customs regulations frequently change, so check before you leave.

> **Tip:** If you are going through to another destination and cannot check your luggage until later, you can leave your baggage at the MAS baggage service office.

If you need some Malaysian dollars for a taxi, there are banks on the arrival level. Check each one for the best rate. If it is late Saturday or Sunday, and you need cash for that day or taxi money for the next morning, get it now because banks will be closed and hotel rates are always bad.

> **Tip:** When you leave you must pay a departure tax. Keep M $5 in reserve for domestic departure. For international departure, keep M $20. Check at your hotel for any possible changes in these amounts.

Getting to the Hotel

Once you are through customs, you can move out into the heat to the taxi queue, which moves quickly. If you are fortunate enough to have an expense account that allowed you to arrange for a hotel car to

An Expedient Arrival in Kuala Lumpur

pick you up, you'll find it costs about U.S. $25. But this service isn't necessary; all the airport cabs are air-conditioned and decent.

Cabs operate on a coupon system. You prepay your fare at the taxi stand in Malaysian dollars and, in exchange, you will be given a coupon or ticket that you present to your cab driver. You must buy your coupon before you get into your cab. The taxi stands are located beside the taxis; you can't miss them.

There is a set charge for the taxi fare from the airport to anyplace downtown, and the rate is listed on a blackboard. A cab from Subang Airport to downtown costs approximately M $20. The drive to the downtown hotel area of Kuala Lumpur takes about 30 minutes from Subang, but if it's raining heavily it could take up to an hour.

> **Tip:** In Sabah and Sarawak, taxis are not metered. Settle on a price before you get in.

5 Highlights of the Major Cities

MAS, Malaysia's airline system, operates daily flights to and from Kuala Lumpur to Kota Kinabalu, Kuching, and other major cities.

Kuala Lumpur

Kuala Lumpur, the Garden City of Lights, is the capital city of Malaysia. It is a cosmopolitan, expanding city, with a population of two million.

Kuala Lumpur, in the State of Selangor, is halfway down the west coast of the peninsula and 35 km (56 mi.) inland. It is 42 km (26 mi.) north of Port Klang, one of Malaysia's major sea ports on the Straits of Malacca, one of the busiest shipping lanes in the world.

Kuala Lumpur lies in the Klang Valley and is bordered to the east by the mountain range that runs through the Malay Peninsula.

The city was founded in 1857 by Chinese tin miners who had come up the Klang River in search of precious tin. They were brought to a halt by shallow water and mud and were forced to stop at the confluence of the Gombak and Klang rivers. There they found nothing but a small village standing in muck. In disgust with this muddy, mucky place, they named the place Kuala Lumpur — muddy confluence. (Today, the Klang and Gombak rivers have been so altered that they are now no bigger than large sewers.)

Later when valuable tin was found upstream, Kuala Lumpur serviced a bustling mining area. Chinese laborers were brought in to mine the tin. By 1860, it was a typical mining town controlled by the Chinese. The large male population attracted get-rich-quick schemers, prostitutes, gambling, and organized crime.

After a civil war, tin prices plunged and the future of Kuala Lumpur looked bleak. The British then took an interest in Kuala Lumpur. In 1882, Frank Swettenham was given the title Resident of Selangor. He had a vision for Kuala Lumpur. He tore down the tin shanties and built a real city with brick buildings, roads, and the Kuala Lumpur-to-Klang railway.

The government's emigration policy in the late nineteenth century, along with encouragement for Bumiputra to own farms, rubber, and coffee plantations, increased Bumiputra (Malay) population and control. The Chinese Malays had to take a back seat. This time, Indian labor was imported to build the railway and work the plantations.

Today, Kuala Lumpur is a multi-racial city, and most neighborhoods, other than Chinatown and the two Indian neighborhoods near the railway of Central and Jalan Tun Sambanthan, are mixed.

The Importance of Kuala Lumpur

Kuala Lumpur became the capital in 1973. In 1972, it attained city status and is now a booming cosmopolitan metropolis.

Kuala Lumpur is the seat of the central government. All important decisions are made there. Accessibility by air, sea, and land has made it the center of commerce and industry. It is linked by road and rail to Singapore in the south and Thailand in the north. Kuala Lumpur is the major stop for anyone looking for opportunities in Malaysia.

A plan to relocate most federal departments to a former rubber estate 60 km (37 mi.) south of Kuala Lumpur and 8 km (5 mi.) north of the new international airport built at Sepang will be fully completed by the year 2000. The relocation will ease traffic congestion in the city.

Kuala Lumpur is gaining international recognition for world class shopping and for its architecture. Just take a look around and you'll see why.

City Patterns

The city is approximately 234 square km (90 square mi.). The business district is spread out in all directions, although nothing is that far away by big city standards.

Jalan Sultan Ismail runs north-south. This is the main modern hotel and central business district street.

The Hilton and the Shangri-La Hotel are located here, as well as the Malaysian Tourist Information Complex.

If you continue north on Jalan Sultan Ismail, you will come to Little India. Some small- to medium-sized accounting and law firms are located here, but they are not necessarily run by Indians.

Imbi Plaza is located at the south end (where Jalan Imbi meets Jalan Sultan Ismail). Imbi Plaza is Kuala Lumpur's computer mall with amazing deals on software and computers. Across the street from the Imbi Plaza is the Park Royal Hotel (formerly the Regent).

Northwest of this area is where the Bank Negara, the Export Trade Centre, and some government buildings are located on Jalan Kuching.

> **Tip:** Traveling time in a taxi from a downtown appointment to a cross-town appointment can take ten to 30 minutes depending on traffic and rain.

Jalan Parlimen, west off Jalan Kuching, leads you to Parliament House. Jalan Kuching continues to Ipoh and the north. In this area off Jalan Kuching and Jalan Raja is the much photographed Sultan Abdul Samad Building. Once the State Secretariat Building, its 41-meter clock tower and curving arches and domes house the High Court.

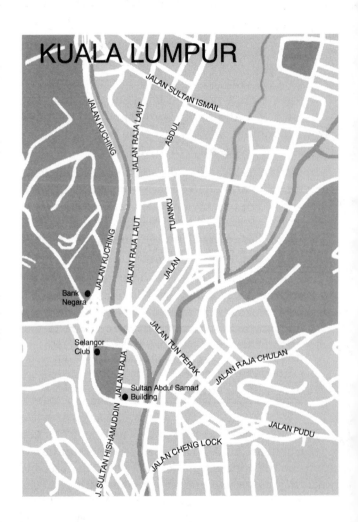

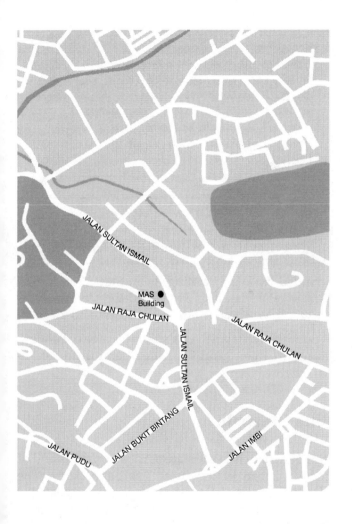

> **Note of interest:** Jalan Kuching starts at a large plaza called Merdeka Square that symbolizes Malaysia's independence. The square boasts the distinction of having the tallest flagpole in the world. An interesting relic from the colonial past is the Selangor Club, located on the fringe.

Chinatown and the Central Market are just east of the Sultan Abdul Samad Building. The landmark building Dayabumi, a futuristic-looking tower, is also here. Chinatown and the Central Market area are bounded by Jalan Petaling, Jalan Sultan, and Jalan Bandar. The Mandarin Hotel and the Malaya Hotel are within walking distance if you can stand the heat.

South down Jalan Syed Putra is the area of Petaling Jaya, Port Klang, and the Kuala Lumpur-to-Seremban Highway.

Kota Kinabalu

Kota Kinabalu is in the state of Sabah on the Island of Borneo. Sabah is known as The Land Below The Wind because it is below the typhoon belt. It has 1,440 km (895 mi.) of coastline, with the Sulu Sea lying to the East and the South China Sea to the West.

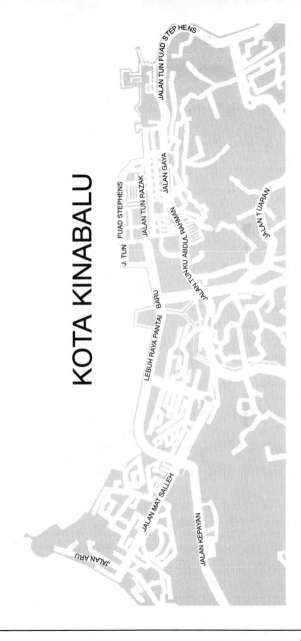

The climate here is tropical with little temperature variation. The maximum temperature is 32°C (90°F) and minimum temperature is 23°C (73°F). Rain is heaviest in December, January, and February.

Sabah and Sarawak together have a population of 3.3 million. The population of Kota Kinabalu population is approximately 14,000.

Kota Kinabalu is an interesting, relatively new city on the South China Sea. The original town was razed during World War II and the new city is well planned and easy to get around. The lifestyle is relaxed and casual.

City transportation is by minibus, regular bus, and taxi. Not all taxis are metered, so ask your desk clerk for approximate prices to be sure you are not overcharged.

The Sepilok Orangutan Sanctuary is on the island of Borneo. These unusual, captivating creatures can be seen, played with, and fed at the sanctuary. Most are young and have been orphaned after illegal poaching killed their mothers.

There are short daily flights from Kota Kinabalu to Sandakan. A short taxi ride and a walk in the jungle will bring you to a spot where you can meet an orangutan, nicknamed "the Wild Man of Borneo."

If you go, wear good shoes and take insect repellent.

Kuching

Kuching is on the northwest coast of Borneo in Sarawak, the largest of the 13 states of Malaysia with a land area of 124,450 square km (48,050 square mi.).

The state of Sarawak is known as the "Land of the Hornbills." It lies underneath Sabah and is bordered on the east by Kalimantan Indonesia and on the west by the South China Sea.

Sarawak's multi-racial population includes over 23 ethnic groups. Approximately 1.6 million people live there. The state is a favorite of the adventure traveler because of its rain forests and Skrang River trips to ethnic villages. Adventurous tourists take trips down the river and stay overnight in a tribal longhouse.

It is big on oil production, timber, gas, rubber, pepper, sago, bird's nest, and copra. Tourism is growing and has tremendous potential for entrepreneurs.

The capital, Kuching, sits on the banks of the Sarawak River, 32 km (20 mi.) from the sea. Its population is 306,000.

> **Note of interest:** An Englishman, James Brooke, was made the Rajah of Sarawak in 1841 for his help in quelling a Sarawak rebellion against the rule of the Brunei sultanate. The family ruled until World War II when Sarawak was invaded by the Japanese. After the war it ceded to Britain. In 1963, Sarawak joined the Federation of Malaysia.

Malaysia's Ports

Malaysia has five major federal ports. Port Klang is the most important harbor and has full facilities for transport.

Also on Peninsular Malaysia, ports are located at Penang, Kuantan, and Johor at Pasir Gudang.

Sarawak is served by Bintulu Port. Bintulu is Malaysia's first liquefied natural gas (LNG) port.

Sabah has Kota Kinabalu Port, which is state regulated.

All these ports are capable of handling both containerized and non-containerized cargo, although Port Klang is the largest.

6 Getting Around with Ease

Taxis

Traveling by taxi is the best choice for transportation in the city. The taxis are air-conditioned, metered, reliable, and easily flagged down.

You can queue in line at a marked taxi stand, flag one down, or call for a cab on the phone. (There is a small surcharge for telephoning.) In Kuala Lumpur, phone 2936211, 2415193, 2211011, 7330507, or 7815352.

Taxis are painted yellow and black or red and white. You can't miss them. Most taxi drivers speak English and are honest and proud of their work.

You can rent taxis by the hour or for the day at all hotels. Rates vary. Unless you are traveling to an area that has a taxi shortage, it is more practical to take taxis as you need them and pay metered fare. Your concierge or desk clerk can advise you. Note that at the airport you must pay for a taxi coupon (a prepayment system for your taxi fare — see chapter 4 for more information).

Taxis always drive you to the exact spot where you should get out, for example the door of the building, not the driveway, even if you have to wait for cars to move. This wastes time and costs you more. Sometimes it is more expedient to get out, walk the few steps, and save time and a little money. Remember you have that option. Make sure the meter is turned turn off as soon as you arrive at your destination.

Tell your driver where you are going before you get in. You can tell by his response if he knows how to get there. Look in the back seat to make sure you will find it comfortable and clean, and don't get in unless you find it up to your standards. Another taxi will soon come along or you can call for one.

You may find it difficult to get a taxi between 3:00 p.m. and 3:30 p.m. because this is when drivers change shifts. It can also be hard to find taxis late at night in Petaling Jaya.

There is a 50% surcharge for cabs between midnight and 6:00 a.m.

There is a small extra charge for more than two passengers. Tips are not expected, but if you do tip, simply round up to the nearest dollar.

Buses

Buses in the city are not suitable for business travelers. They are cheap, but they are hot, crowded, slow, and uncomfortable. The same is true for buses traveling between major cities.

If you do end up taking a bus, be sure to take an express. Only express buses connecting major towns are air-conditioned. Be aware that often the buses are not on schedule.

Kuala Lumpur's main bus station is located at Pudu Raya, near Chinatown (Tel: (03)2300145).

Car Rentals

You can rent a car to drive from one of many local rental agencies. Prices are higher than in North America and vary according to the type of car.

Car insurance is mandatory and an additional charge. Personal insurance is optional. Check your credit cards, as they may cover part of the insurance.

There are a number of rental companies to choose from. Avis is the largest with offices in most cities. Hertz and Budget also operate in Malaysia, and all three companies have offices downtown and at the major airports. To get an idea of the prices before you go, call any of these companies on the toll-free international rental numbers.

From Canada:

- Avis: 1-800-879-2847
- Budget: 1-800-268-8900
- Hertz: 1-800-263-0600

From the United States:

- Avis: 1-800-331-1084
- Budget: 1-800-472-3325
- Hertz: 1-800-654-3131

All companies are reputable, but if you are going out of the city where you rented the car, you are probably better off dealing with Avis because it has the most offices. If your car happens to break down, you can be assured of a getting a replacement car quickly. Avis also seems to have the best selection of cars.

A reputable local car rental company in Kuala Lumpur is Mayflower. They have a desk on the second floor of the Ming Court Hotel. Kasina Rent A Car, another local company, has its office in the Federal Hotel, and National Rent A Car operates out of the Park Royal Hotel.

Telephone numbers in Kuala Lumpur:

- Avis: (03)2423500
- Budget: (03)2425006
- Hertz: (03)2486433
- National: (03)2480522
- Mayflower: (03)2611136
- Kasina: (03)2449968

All types of cars are available: small, mid-size, full-size, and luxury. And all come in manual or automatic (but automatics cost a little more). The small car that is rented by all companies is the Malaysian-manufactured Proton Saga. This tiny car gives you good gas mileage. If you want a lot of space, Toyota and Nissan minibuses are available, as well as everything in between.

> **Tip:** Check on corporate and Automobile Association rates. Save yourself some money and pay with your credit card if it has free auto rental collision/loss damage insurance.

Driving in Malaysia

Malaysia is an easy country to drive in. In other Asian countries, renting a car often means renting a driver as well, but this is not so in Malaysia. The roads are well marked and clear. (Driving is on the left-hand side of the road.) You can purchase road maps at any petrol (gas) station.

> **Tip:** You will want to avoid driving down the coast during monsoon season. We have driven through Malaysia a number of times, and the only difficulties we have ever encountered were heavy rains and flooding when we crossed to Singapore.

The country's excellent road system spans 30,000 km (18,645 mi.). The causeway connects Peninsular Malaysia and Singapore, then goes up the west coast to the border of Thailand. From there, two highways run across the peninsula to the east coast. The new North South Expressway is a multi-lane highway running from Singapore to Penang.

Most highway signs are international, but watch for these:

Awas — Caution

Berhenti — Stop

Jalan sehala — One-way street

Ikut kiri — Keep left

Kurangkan laju — Slow down

Utara — North

Selatan — South

Timur — East

Barat — West

> **Tip:** The law requires drivers and front-seat passengers to wear their seat belts. Fines of up to M $200 or a prison term of up to six weeks can be imposed for infractions.

Keep small change for the toll roads. Tolls run from 50 sen to a couple of ringgit.

The speed limit in towns is 50 kmh (30 mph). The limit varies outside towns; watch for signs. On some roads, there are no speed limits.

Petrol (gas) is quite cheap. You can find stations in and at the edge of all towns. A few are open 24 hours, but to be safe make it a habit to fill up before 10:00 p.m.

Malaysian highway drivers use the following safety signals:

- If the car in front of you flashes its right indicator, it means "do not pass."
- If the car in front of you flashes its left indicator, it means "pass with caution."
- If the car driver flashes the headlights, he or she is taking the right of way.
- In traffic circles or roundabouts, the driver to the right has the right of way.

Parking in Kuala Lumpur is easy. Both metered parking and parking lots are available. If you are approached by young people asking for a few ringgit to watch your car, pay them. It's not worth risking vandalism if you don't.

Be sure to obtain an international driver's license before you go.

Trains

If you want to travel by train, you'll find the prices reasonable and the scenery worth experiencing. It is also relatively comfortable if you book first class, which has air-conditioned cabins and sleepers.

There are two lines for passenger service: north from Singapore through Kuala Lumpur and Butterworth, ending at the Thailand border, and from Gemas on the west coast to the northeast part of the peninsula near Kota Bharu. Both lines link with the Thai railway line at the border. There are trains that do the "milk run" as well as express trains that stop only at major towns.

Call your Malaysian Tourism Office ahead of time for schedules. Also check for Visit Malaysia Rail Passes, which are good value and available only to foreigners. In Kuala Lumpur, call the railway station at (03)2747435.

Ferry Service

Regular boat service is available between Lumut-Pangor Island, Kuala Perlis-Langkawi Island, and Mersing-Tioman Island.

There is a 24-hour ferry service from Butterworth to Penang Island. Tickets can be purchased at the Butterworth Terminal.

Airline Travel

If you want to cover long distances in the shortest time, take a plane. It is the only logical way to travel to Sabah and Sarawak. Malaysian Airlines (MAS) has a good record of air safety and provides good service to all Malaysian destinations. A second option is the smaller domestic carrier, Pelangi Air.

When you're in Kuala Lumpur, contact:

- MAS: (03)2610555/2748734 or (03)2624448 (24 hours)

- Pelangi Air: (03)2624448

Thai International, Singapore Airlines, and Royal Brunei also service some Malaysian destinations including Kuala Lumpur. You can book directly or through any travel agent.

Air fares are reasonable and often special rates are available; some include hotel or resort stays. Many of these are three- to five-day excursion specials to resort areas that cost much less than if you book your hotel and flight separately.

> **Tip:** MAS sometimes offers five-coupon Visit Malaysia Air passes that can come in handy for businesspeople who need to travel to five places, or who want to use one destination for a holiday long weekend.

7 An Economic Overview for Business

Malaysia appears to be a country of contradictions. In downtown Kuala Lumpur, you'll see ultra-modern skyscrapers from the central core to the far reaches of the city. These buildings house offices that design and sell the world's most sophisticated computer hardware and state-of-the-art software. Malaysia is the world's third largest manufacturer of computer equipment and is the highest per capita computer supplier in the world. Industry is at the cutting edge of development in Malaysia.

But these same buildings are being constructed by workers whose methods haven't changed for decades. You can see them, high up on bamboo scaffolding using outdated mortar mixers with cement and lime. These are the same methods Malaysians have used in their villages for generations.

In contrast, modern Malaysian businesspeople are stylishly dressed, often holding the latest cellular telephone in one hand and a designer leather briefcase in the other.

> **Note of interest:** One of the world's tallest buildings is located in Kuala Lumpur. The Petronas Towers (the country's national oil and gas company) will stand 442.5 meters (479 feet) above the ground when it is completed in 1997.

Economic Growth

Malaysia's economy has grown at record-breaking levels since the deep recession of the early 1980s. In 1990, Malaysia reached double digit growth for the first time since the 1970s. Estimates for the 21st century are anticipated to be in the range of 7%, having averaged 9% for each of the five years up to the mid-1990s. The manufacturing sector is expected to hold the average up, with projected annual growth at approximately 11% per annum.

Malaysia is currently one of only two countries in the world where economic growth exceeds 8% per annum and inflation is under 4%.

Sixth Malaysia Plan

The government's Sixth Malaysia Plan, released in June, 1991, set out the objectives for national economic development. In a nutshell, the intention is to diversify Malaysia's industrial base by promoting and encouraging technological modernization. The idea is also to provide greater employment opportunity for the Bumiputra Malaysians while reducing any inequities or imbalances among industrial sectors and regions of the country.

Vision 2020

The objectives of the Sixth Malaysia Plan are continued further in Prime Minister Mahathir's Second Outline Perspective Plan 1991-2000 with particular emphasis on his Vision 2020. His vision is to have Malaysia become an advanced, developed country by the year 2000.

Tip: By diversifying Malaysia's industrial base away from its reliance on electronics and following Singapore's successful lead of developing biotechnology and advanced materials technology, Malaysia has created many opportunities for consultants and service providers in these specialized fields. Local Malaysian companies are interested in joint ventures or strategic alliances with western companies and/or individuals able to provide the necessary sophisticated technology. Human resource firms that specialize in this sector will be needed in Malaysia.

This will be achieved by giving high priority to human resource development, thus ensuring an adequate supply of well-trained and educated workers.

Emphasis will be placed on the Bumiputra as it is the government's intent to increase Malay ownership from the current 20% level to 30%.

> **Note of interest:** The World Competitiveness Report on Technological Strategies ranks Malaysia fifth within the NIE's (Newly Industrialized Economies) just behind Singapore, Taiwan, Hong Kong, and South Korea.

MASSA

MASSA, or Malaysia South-South Association, originally called the Malaysia Latin American Association, was officially launched by Prime Minister Mahathir on November 18, 1991. It changed its name the following year to more accurately reflect its target markets.

The objective of the association is to establish strong trading links with non-traditional trading partners in the developing world or so-called "south." Dr. Mahathir originally targeted the emerging Americas, following his successful trade mission to South America and Mexico in 1991. He quickly widened the association's target markets to include Albania, Argentina, Bangladesh, Brazil, Chile, China, the Czech Republic, India, Iran, Mexico, Vietnam, and various African nations. Malaysia is at the upper level of developing nations and will be able to capitalize on its success story when creating strategic alliances with these emerging countries.

MASSCORP, the business operating arm of MASSA, has the objective of promoting Malaysian trade and investment in the developing world. One example is a 300-hectare (750-acre) industrial park in Da Nang, Vietnam. The industrial park being developed by MASSCORP is to be shared with other Malaysian companies wanting to do business in Vietnam.

The members of MASSA read like a "who's who" of Malaysian business. Its member companies have a combined annual turnover of almost U.S. $10 billion, and are very well positioned to take advantage of any joint venture opportunities.

Tariffs

Malaysia is an important member of the six-nation ASEAN (Association of Southeast Asian Nations). The other member countries are Brunei, Indonesia, Thailand, the Philippines, and Singapore.

In 1992, ASEAN formed AFTA, the ASEAN Free Trade Area. Its objective is to open the doors of trade among the six countries and their 340 million people. The average growth rate for the ASEAN countries' economies is 6%, with a total GDP exceeding M $430 billion. Tariffs on as much as 85% of goods traded within ASEAN members are to drop to between 0% and 5% by the year 2003.

The ASEAN countries also make up an important part of the membership of APEC (Asia Pacific Economic Cooperation), which is comprised of Australia, New Zealand, China, Japan, Hong Kong, Taiwan, South Korea, the United States, Canada, Mexico, Papua New Guinea, Chile, and the six ASEAN countries. APEC takes the concept of free trade agreements to almost the whole world, with the exception of the European community.

> **Note of interest:** Following Prime Minister Mahathir's visit to Mexico in 1991, Malaysia's relationship with Mexico really started. Malaysian Airlines added Mexico City to its Los Angeles run, opening the door for businesspeople from both countries. This was consistent with Mahathir's vision of South-South trade relations, MASSA.

Inflation

For the mid-1990s, inflation is currently at 4% in Malaysia. Local experts suggest inflation of closer to 5% will continue into the beginning of the 21st century. Domestic inflation is being kept down by strong economic growth, large capital inflow from foreign investors, and a tight monetary policy from Bank

Negara (the National Bank). Bank Negara's stand is to keep the currency stable relative to the U.S. dollar.

Former Maybank Chief Executive Ahmad Don became Bank Negara's Governor in 1993. Since then the central bank has relied on a policy of a stronger ringgit rather than high interest rates to fight inflation. This has worked well and has kept inflation at 4% while experiencing an 8% growth in the economy.

Malaysia's annual current account deficit is about U.S. $5 billion. The debt service ratio was 9% for 1993. Malaysia is committed to paying on time.

Average Income

Part of the Second Outline Perspective Plan is to have annual per capita income of M $10,200, and a population reaching 70 million by the year 2095. Unlike most countries, Malaysia is encouraging its people to have larger families. The rationale for this unconventional policy is to increase the domestic market, so that it can sustain the industrial sector.

Currency

Bank Negara is serious about maintaining the stability of its currency in relation to the U.S. dollar. When international currency speculators started buying ringgit on a giant scale to raise the value, Bank Negara manipulated the value down, costing the speculators millions!

The ringgit is anticipated to stay in the general vicinity of M $2.50 to U.S. $1.

Employment

Malaysia's population of 18 million people has a labor force of seven million. It is estimated that the labor force will grow at the rate of 3% a year. The Malaysian Institute of Economic Research suggests that the country will need a labor force of 23.3 million by the year 2020. If not, the productivity rate of U.S. $5,000 per worker will have to reach U.S. $22,000 to make up for the lack of labor.

The Human Resources Development Fund was started to help the private sector develop skilled workers. Over 4,500 companies contribute 1% of each employee's wages to the fund every month. To encourage employers to train their employees, the government is matching the 1% employer contribution.

Infrastructure

No matter what corner of the world you talk about, when it comes to emerging markets, infrastructure presents itself as probably the biggest opportunity. Malaysia is no exception. During the 1960s, Malaysia (as well as Thailand and Indonesia) poured millions into its rural infrastructure. Malaysia paved its roads and strung hydro lines into every village to win the peasants back from Communist insurgents.

An Economic Overview for Business

During the Sixth Malaysia Plan, infrastructure spending was up 63% from the previous five years. Transport has been upgraded heavily in the last few years, especially for road and rail projects. A highway running along the east coast of Peninsular Malaysia has been built, and a new international airport being built south of Kuala Lumpur at Sepang will help alleviate some of the traffic congestion at Subang International Airport. With increased manufacturing and exporting, the three major ports in Johor, Klang, and Penang have been running at maximum capacity and are expanding rapidly to keep up with container traffic demands.

> **Tip:** High levels of manufacturing have put a strain on Malaysia's power supply. The government has planned a hydro electric project in Sarawak that will generate up to four times the country's daily power requirements. This energy source will have to be transferred by water to Peninsular Malaysia. Keep an eye on Tenaga Nasional for opportunities.

> **Tip:** Telecom Malaysia is spending almost U.S. $5 billion to install a fiber-optic cable network in Peninsular Malaysia. To accommodate the increased local demand, telephone lines are being expanded. As the population continues to grow, more telecommunications services will be needed.

> **Note of interest:** Binariang Sdn. Bhd. paid U.S. $850 million to Hughes Aircraft for two satellites. The company plans to invest another U.S. $1.34 billion to set up Malaysia's first satellite system, a digital cellular phone network and a national and international telephone network. Malaysia East Asia Satellite (Measat-1) will probably be launched in 1995 or 1996. Prime Minister Mahathir has criticized the western control of media in Asia and has often used Rupert Murdoch's Hong Kong-based Star TV as an example. The Prime Minister hopes Measat will help build a more representative Asian broadcasting network and protect his country's cultural and social integrity. Previously the Prime Minister had been hesitant about licensing television broadcasting rights because of these concerns.

Consumerism

Malaysia is considered an upper-income nation, with all the associated expectations of its consumers. Malaysians love to shop. With incomes on the rise creating greater discretionary income, Malaysia is truly a marketer's dream come true. Consumers, influenced by western television programs such as *Dallas* and *Lifestyles of the Rich and Famous*, demand a wide range of commodities and services previously unavailable in Malaysia. As a result, the last few years have seen consumer-driven growth in service areas such as food, recreation, and financial services.

> **Tip:** If you have any consumer-based product that can be marketed effectively, Malaysia and its eager consumers may be the place for you. Malaysia's population is young, with 45% of the people under the age of 25.

Malaysian consumers recognize the strength of their economy and aren't afraid to go out and spend on consumer goods. According to government reports, families expect their finances to keep improving and plan to spend even more. New cars, stereos, televisions, VCRs, and home improvements are at the top of their list.

> **Note of interest:** Between 1980 and 1992, the number of households in emerging countries, such as Malaysia, that owned a television increased 153% compared to an increase of only 21% in developed countries. Where would you rather be selling TV sets and related equipment?

This ever-increasing wealth, in particular within the middle class, presents giant opportunities for developing personal investment products. Package investments, such as unit trusts (mutual funds), would be easily marketed to the increasingly affluent Malaysian. The Malaysian stock market was set up in 1989. The government then ruled that Malaysian companies were to be removed from the Singapore exchange and list only on Malaysian exchanges. The main exchange is the Kuala Lumpur Stock Exchange (KLSE).

Manufacturing

During the Sixth Malaysia Plan and the Second Outline Perspective Plan, manufacturing is projected to increase its share in the GDP from 27% in 1990 to 80% of total exports by 2000. This would replace agricultural exports such as rubber (Malaysia is the world's largest producer) and timber, which represents 9% of total exports.

The electrical and electronics industry is the largest part of the manufacturing sector. Malaysia is a major manufacturer of semiconductors and electronic components, radio and television sets, and other electrical goods and cables and wires. Malaysia has also become one of the world's largest exporters of room air conditioners and semiconductors. (The price of pig iron used to be an economic indicator, now semiconductors are considered a more accurate thermometer of an economic climate!)

An Economic Overview for Business

> **Note of interest:** According to the 1992 World Competitiveness Report, Malaysia ranked fourth in international competitiveness among developing and newly developed economies, with only Singapore, Hong Kong, and Taiwan placing higher. When considering Malaysia as a manufacturing location, it is encouraging to know that Malaysia received high recognition for basic research, technological advancement, long-term competitiveness, and old-fashioned hard work.

> **Tip:** The government is very receptive to helping manufacturers expand their operations and whenever possible encourages team work between local industries and foreign investors and businesses.

The Federation of Malaysian Manufacturers (FMM) is an efficiently managed chamber of commerce and is highly effective as the representative voice of Malaysian manufacturers. The federation takes an active role with the government regarding budget and economic issues. FMM provides useful information to local members and valuable assistance to foreign investors.

> **Note of interest:** In recent years, Japan has shifted its focus from the highly industrialized and competitive markets of North America to the fast-growing, large economies and large population area of Asia, particularly southeast Asia. Japanese investment in Malaysia only started to any great extent after 1987. By 1994, there were 150 Japanese companies doing business in Malaysia. According to a survey in September, 1994, by the Japanese Chamber of Trade and Commerce in Malaysia (Jactim), more than 35 of its 150 members were planning to list on the Kuala Lumpur Stock Exchange over the next 12 months, with many other companies giving serious consideration to a public offering. New initial public offerings of this caliber will attract more equity investors and help prolong the growth the Malaysian stock market has enjoyed during the 1990s.

Mining

Tin is Malaysia's major mining export. Malaysia used to be the world's largest exporter of tin, however, tin production fell 47% in 1994 while local demand for the metal increased by 4%.

Australian mining concerns have been the main foreign player in Malaysian mining activity. But, with falling world prices, the mining sector may slow down further.

> **Tip:** Many mining companies have been watching and participating in the growth of Latin America. Malaysia and other parts of southeast Asia offer even greater potential for the entrepreneurial mining company and specialist. These countries will require foreign assistance in transportation, telecommunications, energy, electricity, mining, agriculture, and forestry management, creating opportunities for companies and individuals prepared to invest the time and resources.

Oil and Gas

Petronas is the government-run petroleum company. It has had successful joint ventures with companies such as Shell, Mitsubishi, and others. Malaysia has increased its supply of oil and liquefied natural gas and is now a net exporter of these commodities. The main location for exploration is in East Malaysia (Sarawak) and off the west coast of Peninsular Malaysia.

In 1994, Petronas made a major discovery off the coast of Vietnam near Vung Tau which appears to have substantial reserves. Malaysia also lays claim to exploratory rights in the Spratly Islands off the coast of Vietnam, along with China, Brunei, the Philippines, Indonesia, and Vietnam.

Agriculture

Agriculture still plays a big part in the economy, albeit a declining one. In the mid-1990s, palm oil, rubber, and timber represented approximately 23% of total exports. Malaysia is the world's largest producer of palm oil, and as far back as the 1800s it has set the pace globally for production and export of rubber. These days rubber production is down due to lower worldwide demand and Malaysia's increasing labor costs.

Sabah and Sarawak are the largest providers of raw timber within Malaysia and Peninsular Malaysia produces the most sawed timber. Sabah and Sarawak will soon catch up as they expand their lumber mills and timber treatment facilities.

Malaysia is realizing the importance of creating a level of secondary production in processing raw material, whether it is palm oil, timber, or rubber. The government promotes the processing of natural resources to a more finished product before selling overseas.

8 Special Economic Zones

Traditionally, industries have concentrated around urban centers, which has slowed the development of rural communities. The Malaysian government now tries to encourage industries to establish operations throughout the country by offering tax incentives to those that locate in less-developed areas.

The government has also set up a number of special economic zones to encourage different facets of industry to develop throughout the country. Both free trade zones and industrial estates encourage the widespread growth of the economy.

Free Trade Zones

There are a number of free trade zones throughout Malaysia.

These are areas specially designed for manufacturers who produce or assemble products for export.

Free trade zones allow export-oriented industries to enjoy minimum customs control and formalities. This applies to both imported raw materials, parts, machinery, equipment, and the export of the finished products.

> **Tip:** Products exported from free trade zones are free of customs duty. If your market is outside Malaysia, manufacturing in one of the free trade zones could be the best deal for you.

Establishing a manufacturing project in one of these zones is particularly attractive for companies that export between 80% and 100% of their production. Industries that use Malaysian mineral and agricultural resources, or companies that export most or all of their local production, receive preferred incentives.

Industries that import a large portion of their raw materials are also eligible to set up in a free trade zone. The government prefers that local raw materials are used.

Industrial Estates

Industrial estates have been established and continue to be planned in all parts of the country to serve the needs of the manufacturing sector. The government provides the basic infrastructure of roads, water, power, and telecommunications facilities. There are approximately 200 industrial estates throughout Malaysia. Most are located in the states of Selangor, Penang, Perak, and Johor.

Selangor

The industrial estates in Selangor have always been a preferred location because of their proximity to Kuala Lumpur, Subang International Airport, and Port Klang, the largest seaport in the country.

Historically, Selangor's industrial estates specialized in light-to-heavy industries. The Selangor State Development Corporation has been instrumental in the development of these industries, especially in Petaling Jaya, Shah Alam, Setapak, and other estates.

Industry is now shifting toward high tech production following the success of electronic and electrical industrial estates, such as Selat Kelang Utara.

Penang

Penang is a clearinghouse for Malaysia's wealth. Penang's port trades in tin, rubber, copra, oil, rice, timber, and palm oil.

With a modern telecommunications network, international banking and high tech industries thrive. Penang has its own international airport and an adequate railway and highway system that links it to Kuala Lumpur, Singapore, and Bangkok. Its sophisticated infrastructure has attracted multinational corporations to make Penang their base.

> **Note of interest:** Penang has been an important port since August 11, 1786, when Francis Light of the British East India Company took possession of the island and established the first British settlement in the Far East.

> **Tip:** The success of Penang's high tech industrial estates creates more opportunities for service and support companies.

Perak

Perak is geographically positioned to benefit from development in Selangor to the south and Penang next door. The Ipoh Cargo Terminal, Malaysia's first inland port, allows the State of Perak shipping access to Port Klang, Pasir Gudang in Johor, and Penang Port.

> **Tip:** The islands off the coast of Perak, Pangkor, and Pangkor Laut (Little Pangkor), offer very pleasant accommodation. Both islands provide a great getaway after doing business in Kuala Lumpur or one of the industrial estates. Depart from Lumut by ferry.

Johor

Johor is the country's fastest growing state, and the most popular for foreign investors. It is the closest Malaysian state to Singapore and is perfectly positioned geographically to benefit from trade with Singapore and Batam Island. The Johor State Economic Development Corporation encourages the development of high tech industrial estates. Singapore's development in biotechnology and other advanced sciences has helped lead the way for Malaysia to expand into these areas.

> **Note of interest:** Investors consider Johor, Singapore, and Batam Island as one region rather than three separate ones: Singapore for its sophisticated communications, finance, and high technology, and Johor and Batam for their cost-efficient cheap labor and tax incentives. Pasir Gudang is the port near Johor Bahru. The success of local industrial estates means that Johor's port is being used to capacity. Many exporters use the ports of Singapore, which can handle the overload more efficiently than Pasir Gudang.

> **Tip:** Johor has also benefited from capital-intensive projects, such as petrochemical and steel-making factories. The state government is very proactive. Trade missions are regularly sent to Japan, Taiwan, South Korea, and elsewhere to find investors for the establishment of light, medium, or heavy industries.

Labuan for Entrepreneurs

One of the real pleasures of doing business in this part of the world is the opportunity to get in on the ground floor of developments and projects. Labuan is one of these exciting opportunities.

Labuan is made up of seven small islands located just off the coast of Sabah, 123 km (76 mi.) from Kota Kinabalu. Until 1984, Labuan was part of the State of Sabah; now it is a federal territory and is controlled by the federal government of Malaysia.

The main objective of federalizing Labuan was to accelerate the development of the region's economy. This was to be achieved by developing Labuan into a miniature Hong Kong or Singapore, an International Offshore Financial Centre (IOFC). (An IOFC is basically a small territory or jurisdiction that imposes low or no taxes on income, profit, dividends, and interest earned or derived from offshore business activities or transactions.)

The development of an IOFC further enhances Malaysia's attractiveness and competitiveness on an international level. It complements the on-shore financial network and attracts new investors with different requirements. The Malaysian government is motivated to make Labuan work. Acknowledging the healthy competition that exists with Singapore, the government wants Labuan to compete head-on as an IOFC. It favors businesses that support the IOFC, so establishing a regional office in Labuan could open the door for some excellent contacts and strategic alliances with the government and major Malaysian corporations.

Labuan is a perfect site for Malaysia's International Offshore Financial Centre. It is located on the major shipping and air routes of the ASEAN region, and is equidistant from Bangkok, Hong Kong, Jakarta, Manila, and Singapore. It also has daily flights to Kuala Lumpur and other financial capitals.

The growth in Labuan in recent years has been impressive. In 1990, there was very little in the way of amenities. Since then Malaysia has been pouring money into it. Soon to be completed will be a financial park with three high-rise office towers and two condominium blocks. Also planned is a marina center with a hotel, a clubhouse, and berths for luxury, ocean-going yachts.

> **Tip:** Multinational corporations (MNCs) often register their head offices in an IOFC to avoid exchange controls and to minimize taxation. Most IOFCs waive all stamp and death duties, and value-added taxes or inheritance and estate duties usually do not apply. Labuan is designed to be a low-tax jurisdiction. Companies incorporated or registered under the Offshore Companies Act of 1990 are taxed at the reduced rate of 3% of their net trading profits up to a maximum of M $20,000. Income from non-trading activities, such as holding securities, stocks, deposits, and rental income, attracts *no tax*.

> **Tip:** Multinational corporations may want to consider Labuan as a regional base for their administration activities in Southeast Asia. Trading companies registered in Labuan that buy and sell globally would incur very little or no tax. To maximize the benefits of this IOFC, Labuan-registered companies could hold the shares or stock in subsidiary companies and own patents, trademarks, copyrights, and other intellectual property.

IOFCs, and Labuan in particular, were designed with financial institutions in mind. Labuan is well suited for running back-office operations, such as foreign exchange trading, treasury activities, and administration of trusts. Just about any banking function that does not involve retail services can be run efficiently from Labuan.

The Malaysian government wants to set up a Labuan International Monetary Exchange like the financial futures market in Singapore. Also being considered is an international stock exchange where offshore companies could list and trade their shares.

Tip: Labuan provides an excellent opportunity to lend foreign currency to clients in the region. Keep in mind there is no tax on loan portfolios. (Note that residents of Malaysia are not allowed to conduct business with a Labuan registered company unless it involves foreign currency loans or deposits.)

Tip: The Public Bank, one of Malaysia's largest banks, was one of the first to operate in Labuan, offering a full range of services. It also offers a range of investment products to residents of Malaysia. A strategic alliance with such an institution in Labuan could easily lead to joint opportunities on the mainland.

> **Note of interest:** An example of Labuan's ability to raise capital was the U.S. $250 million loan for the Malaysian Highway Authority in 1994. The loan was arranged by Bank Bumiputra and the Maybank along with four Japanese institutions: Daichi Kangyo Bank, IBJ, Sumitomo Bank, and Tokai Bank. The Japanese banks previously obtained financing from Singapore.

Tip: The international accounting firm KPMG (Klynveld, Peat Marwick, Goerdler) is well represented in Malaysia and also has an office in Labuan. KPMG can be of great assistance in researching and establishing trusts or companies in Labuan.

9 Joint Ventures and Doing Your Business

Malaysia offers a stable and conducive investment environment for foreign investors. The country is eager to benefit from foreigners manufacturing or providing technical expertise and offering a variety of incentives and tax concessions. The doors are open to new capital and export markets.

> **Tip:** Many foreign investors who want to establish an ongoing business in Malaysia set up private limited companies under the Companies Act 1965. Private limited companies can be set up with local partners who have varying levels of ownership, or companies can be wholly owned by the foreign investor. Tax concessions and business incentives for foreign investors are only available to locally registered companies.

When developing local industries, the Malaysian government prefers projects to be undertaken on a joint venture basis. The government can be flexible if the foreign company's venture will be limited to a specific project or if the project is substantially export-oriented. Otherwise, the government insists that a business establish a local subsidiary or enter into a joint venture with a local Malay operation.

Malaysian Investment Development Agency (MIDA)

The Malaysian Investment Development Agency (MIDA) has the ultimate say about whether a project can be developed in Malaysia and what level of majority ownership is allowed. MIDA decisions on what projects or joint ventures will be allowed are based on details relating to each individual proposal. Approvals on projects can be obtained within two months. With pressure, two to three weeks is possible.

MIDA has a reputation for being efficient and can be incredibly useful. Contact MIDA before your first business trip or when you arrive in Kuala Lumpur. MIDA will assist with introductions to a compatible business. Take a look at MIDA's directory, *Your Potential Partner for Joint Ventures in Malaysia*. You can order one by fax or by phoning your closest MIDA office.

Non-Resident Controlled Company (NRCC)

A Non-Resident Controlled Company (NRCC) is supposed to obtain at least 60% of its credit requirements from local financial institutions. NRCCs are encouraged by the government to finance their projects with as much of their own funds as possible.

NRCCs are allowed to borrow up to M $10 million from any source within Malaysia without having to obtain government approval. Loans that exceed this amount require permission from the Controller of Foreign Exchange, who works in the Bank Negara, Malaysia's national bank.

Approval is based on the genuine needs of the company, the level of shareholder equity, the amount of long-term foreign loans outstanding, and the current credit situation of the country.

Joint Venture Rules

- A local partner is not required for projects that involve the manufacture of goods where 80% of production is exported.
- For projects that export 50% or more, but less than 80% of their production, foreign equity ownership of up to 100% can be allowed under certain circumstances where manufactured goods do not compete with anything that is locally manufactured and the foreign investor

invests a minimum M $50 million in fixed assets, excluding real estate.
- Other export-oriented joint venture projects will allow foreign ownership of up to 51%, as long as 51% to 79% of production is exported.
- For projects that export 20% to 50% of their production, foreign equity ownership of between 30% and 51% will be allowed.
- Any project exporting less than 20% of production will be restricted to a maximum of 30% foreign ownership.

Note: Projects producing high technology products or priority products for the domestic market will be allowed foreign ownership of up to 51%.

Tip: The government is eager to develop and assist the Bumiputras in every possible way, which makes for excellent joint venture opportunities. For example, the Bumiputra Unit Trust has a data base of over one million clients and the Bank Bumiputra Malaysia Berhad is one of the largest banks in Malaysia. Organizations like these represent golden opportunities for developing retail investment/savings and insurance products tailored to the needs of the Bumiputra population, such as education funding and health insurance.

The Local Partner

When foreign equity is less than 100%, the balance has to be taken up by Malaysians. If the foreign investor does not have a local partner identified, the balance of the equity will be taken up by Bumiputra investors. If less than 70% of the equity is held by foreigners, 30% will be reserved for Bumiputra and the balance for non-Bumiputra. If foreign investors aren't careful, they can end up with a number of partners!

> **Tip:** If you have identified a local partner who is not a Bumiputra, and you do not want a Bumiputra participating in the project, have your non-Bumiputra partner initiate the joint venture proposal. If the foreign equity is greater than 70%, you will have no problem maintaining ownership between the two of you. However, if foreign equity is less than 70%, your non-Bumiputra partner will hold 30% and the balance will be allocated to other Bumiputra investors. Under special circumstances, the non-Bumiputra may be allowed to take up the entire balance of the equity. Obtain permission from the Ministry of International Trade and Industry (MITI).

Note: Joint venture and investment regulations can change at a moment's notice. Please check with MIDA for the most current rules and regulations.

Privatization

An active program of privatization has been underway in Malaysia since 1986. Among government-owned entities that were privatized and then listed on the KLSE are Malaysian Airlines, a national shipping company, and telecommunications and utilities companies.

> **Tip:** Foreign investors with expertise in industries the government wants to privatize are encouraged to participate in privatization projects. The entrepreneur who can identify the next industry to be deregulated or privatized will have the greatest opportunity.

Income Tax

Generally, all incomes of companies or individuals are taxed. Along with income tax, there is a type of capital gains tax, a sales tax, and a service tax. Income from foreign sources is not subject to tax unless and until it is brought back to Malaysia by the resident.

All residents are liable for income tax on income earned in Malaysia. A resident is taxed on total income at progressive rates from 2% to 34% after allowing for tax deductions (or tax reliefs as they are referred to in Malaysia).

An individual's resident status is determined by the duration of his or her stay in the country. Most short-term visitors receive a tax exemption on income derived in Malaysia when their presence does not exceed 60 days per calendar year.

Non-resident individuals may have their incomes taxed at fixed rates ranging from 15% to 35% depending on the nature of their activity. Generally tax reliefs are not available to non-residents.

Company Tax

A company, whether resident or not, pays tax on income earned in Malaysia. Foreign income earned by Malaysian resident companies is also taxable. A company is considered a resident of Malaysia if control and management (board of directors' meetings) are handled in the country.

Both resident and non-resident companies are taxed at the rate of 34%, except for exploration companies which may incur a tax rate of 45%. These tax rates do not take into account special tax incentives available to many companies.

Tax Incentives

There is a wide variety of incentives for Malaysian-incorporated companies including tax holidays for pioneer companies, investment tax allowances, and benefits for setting up in a promoted industrial area.

The main tax incentives are listed in the Promotion of Investments Act 1986 and the Income Tax Act of 1967. The incentives, like tax rates, can be subject to change. The incentives are designed to make doing business in Malaysia more attractive and to provide tax relief, particularly in a company's start-up years.

Pioneer Status

Pioneer status can be given to companies in the manufacturing sector. A company given pioneer status will be granted partial tax exemption for five years.

Most companies that are granted pioneer status will only have to pay tax on 30% of their income. Companies involved in strategic projects of national importance can receive tax relief of up to 100%.

Investment Tax Allowance

A company given an Investment Tax Allowance (ITA) will be granted an allowance of between 60% and 100% of qualifying capital expenditure in the first five years. The allowance can be used to offset against 70% of income in the year of assessment. Any unused allowance can be carried forward for subsequent years until it is all used up.

The eligibility for either pioneer status or investment tax allowance is determined by the Minister of International Trade and Industry.

Export Incentives — Double Deductions

Many export allowances were abolished in 1994. However, for premium payments made for export credit insurance, a double tax deduction is allowed. This benefit is continued to encourage exporters to penetrate non-traditional markets.

Double deductions are also allowed for the overseas promotion of exports. Some expenses that qualify for a double deduction by Malaysian resident companies are overseas advertising, exhibits and/or participation in trade shows approved by MITI, fares for overseas business travel by employees, meals, and lodging up to certain maximums and more.

Double Taxation

Double taxation agreements prevent the incidence of double taxation on international income. Business profits, dividends, or royalties earned in one country yet received in another could incur double taxation if there were no tax treaty between the two countries.

Comprehensive double taxation agreements exist between many countries, including Canada, Australia, the United States (a limited agreement relating to shipping and air transport), New Zealand, most western European nations, Japan, ASEAN members, China, and others.

10 Banks, Investments, and Financial Services Opportunities

Banking

Banking, like other sectors of the economy, has experienced a consumer-driven boom. It has been one of the fastest growing industries in the Malaysian economy since the early 1980s.

Foreign Banks

Foreign banks conducting business in Malaysia that are interested in taking advantage of the potentially lucrative retail market must find local partners. Under Malaysian law, foreign banks cannot operate more than one branch without having a local partner. This restricts foreign banks to the corporate and commercial sector with very limited retail potential. Some of the foreign banks that operate in Malaysia include Citibank, Deutsche Bank, Hong Kong Shanghai

Banking Corporation (HSBC), Standard Chartered Bank, and Bank of Nova Scotia.

> **Note of interest:** Bank of Nova Scotia has been operating in Malaysia since 1973. According to the bank, their Malaysian branch has been one of the 15 most profitable branches in the world. To maximize the potential of the Malaysian market, they are teaming up with Idris Hydraulic (Malaysia) Sdn. Bhd.'s finance company subsidiary Kewangan Usaha Bersatu Berhad (KUBB).

Tip: Foreign banks wanting to set up in Southeast Asia should consider establishing a representative office in Kuala Lumpur, which would be an excellent starting point and a convenient hub for future business development in the region. Initially lacking a full commercial banking license, opportunities would still exist for correspondent banking, and *inter alia* (channeling trade business through your office and developing business ties for corporate clients back home). The National Bank of Australia has enjoyed success in Malaysia in this way.

The Central Bank

The Central Bank of Malaysia, Bank Negara, is similar to all central banks and is responsible for issuing the country's currency and maintaining reserves. Bank Negara acts as an adviser to the Malaysian government in its efforts to stabilize the ringgit and ensure that the credit balance of the country remains in check.

The Central Bank maintains control of foreign exchange, including administering and enforcing exchange control regulations. All financial institutions, including money and foreign exchange brokers, merchant and commercial banks, and finance companies are supervised and regulated by Bank Negara.

Local Banks

The commercial banks are the largest and most important players in the finance sector. Its services are as modern and comprehensive as you would find anywhere.

The Maybank (Malayan Bank Berhad) is the country's largest and, perhaps, most popular bank. Bank Bumiputra, United Malayan Bank Corp., and Public Bank are three of the next largest commercial banks.

> **Tip:** To develop financial products for the retail market, such as mortgage reduction plans, corporate-brand credit cards, or education funds, establish a strategic alliance or a joint venture with one of these main banks. Their existing networks and credibility will save you millions and a lot of time.

Merchant banks provide a sophisticated wholesale banking service for the corporate sector and large individual clients. They may participate on an equity basis in new ventures and can be called upon to provide seed capital. They also have the ability to handle non-ringgit deposits for foreigners and foreign exchange loans for residents.

> **Note of interest:** Wardley's, a successful funds management company and a division of HSBC, has the joint venture Utama Wardley Berhad. It provides corporate finance and advisory services, investment advice, and management of unit trusts plus other merchant banking services.

Securities Market

Malaysians enjoy a comparatively sophisticated investment marketplace. Bank savings products compete with government savings certificates. The local stock exchange, Kuala Lumpur Stock Exchange (KLSE), is one of the top performers in the world.

On January 24, 1994, Bank Negara imposed a ban on foreign investors from parking their funds in short-term (less than one year), ringgit instruments. This included certificates of deposit, Bank Negara bills, and all forms of private debt securities.

This measure was aimed at stopping foreign investors from trying to manipulate the ringgit, but had a negative impact on the stock market. On August 11, 1994, the ban was lifted. The Malaysian stock market immediately reacted positively to the announcement, ending a seven-month correction that had caused the Kuala Lumpur Composite Index to fall from 1,332.04 on January 5, 1994, to 920.28 on April 5, 1994.

Tip: There are few retail investment advisers. "Remisiers" are brokers who are licensed to deal in securities and they have a mixed reputation. They are often known for boiler room techniques that raise the value of a company's share price.

Malaysians are confident in their securities markets and prefer to invest at home rather than looking for overseas investments in western currencies. Malaysians seem to prefer investing in the KLSE rather than North American or Australian markets. In many western countries currencies are weak, interest rates can be low, and stock markets underperform by comparison.

Tip: If you are setting up a retail or wholesale network for investment products, you should speak to one of the larger investment advisory operations in this region, O.F.S. (Overseas Financial Services). The head office is in West Sussex, U.K., and the administrative office is in Cyprus. Advisory branches are in Thailand, Indonesia, Hong Kong, Malaysia, Botswana, and the Middle East. They are brokers of unit trusts and life insurance products. Funds they promote include Tyndal, Morgan Grenfell, Guinness, James Capel, Rothschild, and others. Funds are usually registered in the Isle of Man or some other tax-sheltered jurisdiction.

Education

Malaysians put a high price on education. More than 10,000 Malaysian students study in Australia, 15,000 in the United States, and approximately 13,000 in

Canada. Many other Malaysian students prefer to study in Europe and other parts of Asia.

Savings for education is the number one goal for all Malaysian families, particularly among the Chinese Malays. If families cannot afford to send their children overseas for a four-year degree, they will send them to a local school for the first two years and to an overseas university for the balance.

An overseas degree is highly respected and sought after. The very wealthy have no difficulty in paying the high cost of their children's education, and the ever-increasing middle class and the Bumiputra will want the same ability to study at an overseas university. They will have to save for it.

> **Tip:** With the great demand for sending students to overseas universities, an opportunity exists to develop an overseas education fund in which Malaysians can invest over a period of time to accumulate enough money to send their children to the universities of their dreams. The fund could have various investment and currency options depending on the country where the student intends to study.

Employers Provident Fund

The Employers Provident Fund (EPF) is Malaysia's pension or retirement fund. It has been modeled after

Singapore's Central Provident Fund, which has been used most effectively to progress Singapore's infrastructure, technology, and employee benefits.

> **Tip:** The EPF is estimated to have approximately M $50 billion in assets with monthly net inflow of M $400 million. Malaysian life insurance companies have been complacent in chasing this business. They have not lobbied to deregulate or privatize the pension industry. Most insurers have been content with their profitable general insurance portfolios and traditional whole life insurance contracts. Others have looked to Australia and the United States, creating joint ventures to improve their technology and market penetration. Banks are beginning to eye the potential of the personal and corporate superannuation market. Strategic alliances are forming between major life insurance companies and banks. A joint venture between a western fund manager or insurance company with expertise in pensions and a local bank, such as the Maybank, would be a dynamic proposition. The government is privatizing more and more industries. Eventually, the EPF and the total pension industry may become available to select private institutions.

In 1994, employers had to contribute 11% of all employees' wages, and employees had to contribute 9% of their wages to the fund. The employer could elect to increase their level of contribution by 4% up to 15% as an employee benefit for senior employees.

Additional employer contributions can be directed to private insurance or pension companies. Individuals are allowed to contribute a maximum amount each year in superannuation or life insurance and are entitled to a tax deduction. (These amounts are increased from time to time by the government). Any middle manager or higher would not normally have the ability to contribute more to superannuation because of the level of compulsory contributions to the EPF.

Note: Private life insurance personal superannuation products have never taken off in Malaysia. Only a small number of individuals are allowed to "top up" their personal superannuation plans.

> **Note of interest:** In late 1994, Singapore's senior finance minister announced that fund managers and investment bankers will have greater access to the large pool of pension funds under government control (the Central Provident Fund). This begins to open up Singapore's CPF to private financial institutions. Many policies and directions taken by Singapore are eventually duplicated in Malaysia; this may be another.

Foreign Exchange

Malaysia has a liberal foreign exchange policy. All foreign currencies can be used for payments, repatriation of capital, remittance of profits, etc., with the exception of South Africa and Israel. No exchange control permission is required for nonresidents to undertake direct or portfolio investment in Malaysia.

Mutual Funds

The world's emerging markets are attracting more and more investor attention. In recent years, the average economic growth of emerging markets, such as Malaysia, have been twice that of developed nations. Investors wanting this type of growth for their own investments should consider the potential of stock markets in emerging countries.

Investors wanting to share in the exciting growth of these countries' stock markets should use Hong Kong or Singapore registered unit trusts or locally registered mutual funds managed by experienced money managers. Direct share investment in stock markets of emerging countries can be difficult for non-residents because of the time delay in buy and sell orders. Obtaining qualified and up-to-date research can also be very difficult.

The exceptional returns from emerging markets like Malaysia are due in part to the high savings and investment rates that support economic growth.

Younger demographics, increased consumer spending, a low-cost, highly productive labor force also play an important role.

> **Tip:** Diversifying investments into a number of emerging countries through a Southeast Asian Regional Fund managed by an experienced money manager can substantially reduce the risk of being exposed to just one individual market. Tiger or Dragon Funds (Southeast Asian Regional funds) can provide substantial returns to investors. There are a number of top-quality fund managers based in Hong Kong, Singapore, Kuala Lumpur, and Jakarta managing regional and individual country funds.

Jardine Fleming Unit Trusts (registered in Hong Kong) offers individual country funds, including Malaysia, Korea, and Hong Kong, plus regional funds. Jardine Fleming manages one-third of the Canadian Global Strategy's Asia Fund along with Rothschild and AsiaInvest.

Thorntons (a member of the Dresdner Bank Group) is based in Hong Kong and offers a range of Tiger and Dragon Regional Funds. Single country funds for Thailand, Malaysia, Indonesia, Singapore, and others are also available. Thorntons manages the Universal Far East Fund for the Canadian group

Mackenzie. Asset allocation of the fund is based on Thorntons' Little Dragons Fund.

Nomura Securities, one of the world's largest investment companies, has offices around the world and is strategically located in Asia. They manage a wide range of regional and single country funds. In Canada, their expert money management can be obtained by investing in AGF Japanese and Asian mutual funds.

You can invest in some of Templeton's listed emerging market mutual funds and specialized funds such as a Vietnam fund on the New York Stock Exchange. For Templeton's open-ended mutual funds, contact a trusted and experienced mutual fund broker.

Note of interest: Sir John Templeton pioneered the concept of investing in emerging markets. For decades his team has scoured the world looking for companies that represent good value and excellent potential. Templeton Emerging Market Funds are traditional top performers and are available in most western countries. Templeton's Emerging Market Funds are managed by Dr. Mark Mobius. Dr. Mobius, based out of Singapore and Hong Kong, spends ten months each year globe trotting. His enviable, yet tiring job is to research emerging and established companies around the world. Templeton's has a joint venture funds management operation in Indonesia called Indonesia Development Fund, managed through Singapore.

11 Best Buys: Sabah and Sarawak

Malaysia does not have the myriad of crafts that Indonesia or Thailand have to offer, but some interesting, good buys can be had.

Around Kuala Lumpur

Silk
Beautiful silks in pastel and vibrant colors can be bought wholesale at De Lot. Their factory is on the east coast in Kuala Terengganu. The silk is too delicate for drapery and furniture coverings, but is suitable for women's clothing.

Pewter
Tumasek Pewter is a younger, more modern version of the famous Selangor Pewter factory at Setapak. Tumasek has a showroom in Kuala Lumpur where the tour buses bring shoppers to see the factory. Shop owners can arrange to buy wholesale.

Address: Lot 16 Jalan Kanan, Taman Kepong, 52100 Kuala Lumpur. Tel: (3)6341225.

> **Note of interest:** Malaysian Pewter is 97% Straits-refined tin and 3% antimony and copper.

Kelantan State

Kelantan State, on the northeast tip of the Malay Peninsula, is the handicraft center of the peninsula. Kota Bharu can be reached by air, bus, or taxi from Kuala Lumpur. One-way fare is approximately M $40 per person.

Silverware

Malaysian hand-beaten silver is a craft of extraordinary beauty. Kota Baru, capital of Kelantan, is the place to buy bowls, tea sets, ice buckets, jewelry, and other interesting objects. Workmanship can be in filigree or repousses (sheet silver hammered into relief).

Factories are on Jalan Sultanah Zainab, the road North to Pantai Cinta Berahi (Beach of Passionate Love) at Kampung Sireh, Kampung Morak, and Kampung Badang.

Songket

Hand-loomed tapestries woven with gold and silver thread can be purchased along the road from Kota Baru to Pantai Cinta Berahi. This cloth makes beautiful evening jackets. East coast women still use the traditional two-paddle floor looms to make this cloth that was once reserved for royalty. The best pieces come from Kelantan State.

Batik

Wall hangings, shirts, sarongs, ties, and everything else you can possibly think of are available from the factories at Kampung Puteh, Kampung Penambang, Kampung Tingkat, Kampung Kijang, and Kampung Badang. These are all close to Kota Baru. Factory hours are usually 10:00 a.m. to 8:00 p.m.

Traditional Woodcarvings, Kites, and Tops

Kites and tops (*wau* and *gasing*) have been around since the sixteenth century and have become an international sport in Malaysia. These items, as well as traditional woodcarvings, can be purchased along the Kota Baru airport road.

Sarawak

Kuching has more than Kota Kinabalu, but neither are brimming with finds. A hard look will bring rewards, but craftspeople other than Sarawak potters don't seem to be all that prolific.

Woven Straw and Bamboo

Nipah palm reeds are woven into modern and traditional sun hats, decorative mats, baskets, etc. Wander through the market and stores in Kuching if you want to find these.

Beadwork

The Dayaks of Sarawak do very intricate bead work in different forms on hats, belts, baskets, necklaces, and headbands. These are worth a look. Just wander through the stores in Kuching.

Pottery

It is worth a special trip to see Chinese and Borneo pottery. Its traditional Sarawak designs are unique and beautiful. Patterns include warriors that stand out in relief and hand-painted horn bills. Find the old Chinese pottery factories on the road to the Kuching airport. (Shipping can be difficult.)

Primitive Art

Interesting and cheap items including blow pipes, wood carvings, bags, beads, mats, old silver coins, and earrings made from teeth and coins are found in antique shops scattered around Kuching.

Among others are Sarawak House at 35 Wayang Street, the Borneo Art Gallery in the Sarawak Plaza, Tan and Sons Handicrafts, 54 Jalan Padungan, Syarikat Permasaran Karyeneka SdnBhd at Lot 87, Rubber Road and the market in the Main Bazaar. Shops seem to be located at Wayang Street and Temple Street.

Shop owners are willing to bargain up to a point.

Shipping

Ask the shop or factory where you buy goods to recommend a shipper. Shipping is easy and as long as you buy a container-full, it is well worth the trip for a wholesaler or retail enterprise.

It is more difficult to find a shipper in Borneo. When we bought a gorgeous Chinese four-foot vase in a factory on the road to the Kuching airport, we had to carry it ourselves.

12 Where to Stay

Kuala Lumpur hotels are high quality and good value.

Malaysian hotels have not been officially classified, but you can expect the same five-star high standards from the Hilton, Regent, Hyatt, and Holiday Inn as you would expect anywhere in the world. Local chains like the Merlin, Shangri-La, and Ming Court are about the same price and standard as the Hilton or Holiday Inn.

Malaysian hotels charge in Malaysian dollars (ringgits.) Very expensive, five-star hotels charge upwards of M $350 (approximately U.S. $140) for a deluxe double room and can go as high as M $2,000 (approximately U.S. $800) for a suite. The rest of the hotels could be rated as quality three- and four-star, and charge around M $200 (approximately U.S. $80) for a double. (This does not include tax and service.)

Prices are subject to change, so please check with your travel agent when booking. If you are in Malaysia when booking your hotel, the Malaysia Tourism Board will get you the best price.

> **Tip:** A Malaysian travel agent, the airline, or your agent at home can often find packages that are cheaper than the daily room rate, especially for golf and resort hotels. The cost of living is one of the lowest of the large Asian cosmopolitan cities. Hotel rates are less than Jakarta and much less than what travelers to Hong Kong, Singapore, or Tokyo have to pay.

A hefty service charge of 10% plus a 5% tax needs to be added to both hotel and restaurants prices. Tipping is completely unnecessary.

Hotel Listings

Hotels that we specially recommend are noted in boldface below. Please note that at the time of writing, Malaysia was undergoing a construction boom. It's hard to keep up with both the new hotels and the golf courses. Contact your travel agent, MAS, or the Malaysian Tourist Board for updated information.

Five-star accommodation is noted (*****). Four stars (****) indicate older and smaller hotels, but still with very good facilities. Three stars indicate more moderately priced accommodation.

Kuala Lumpur and Area

Carcosa Seri Negara　　　　**Recommended*****
Taman Tasik Perdana
Tel: 60 (3)2821888
Fax: 60 (3)2827888
Toll-free U.S. reservations, call: 1-800-421-1490

A very expensive all-suite hotel, operated by the exclusive and top quality Amanresorts. Thirteen luxurious suites in two mansions on a 40-acre garden property that overlooks a lake. Five minutes by car to city center. All amenities including personal 24-hour butler, business center, tennis courts, pool, sauna, and gym. Queen Elizabeth and other royalty have stayed there.

Regent of Kuala Lumpur　　　　**Recommended*****
Jalan Bukit Batang
Tel: 60 (3)2418000
Fax: 60 (3)2421441
Toll-free reservations: (03)8008006

Part of the deservedly famous international chain. Opened in 1989; 469 rooms and suites and five restaurants. The doorways are embossed with a brass "Kris" (double-edged Malay dagger). Located in the center of the business and shopping district, across from the Kuala Lumpur Plaza. Excellent business center, outdoor pool, gym, health club, squash courts. Doctor on call.

Istana Jalan Raja Chulan ★★★★★
Tel: 60 (3)2419988
Fax: 60 (3)2440111

Asian chain in the heart of downtown. Five hundred and sixteen guest rooms with special Mutiara floors offering complementary services like suit pressing. Business center with word processors for rent. Outdoor pool with garden bar, tennis, massage, squash, golf (by arrangement), gym, sauna, steam bath and whirlpool. Six restaurants and three lounges.

Hilton Kuala Lumpur ★★★★★
Jalan Sultan Ismail
Tel: 60 (3)2422122 and 60 (3)2422222
U.S. toll-free: 1-800-445-8667
Fax: 60 (3)2438069

Located minutes from downtown overlooking the Selangor Turf Club. Five hundred and eighty-one guest rooms and two executive floors with own check-in, butler service, and private lounges also includes complimentary breakfast and cocktails. Business center with interpreters and 24-hour fax. Outdoor pool, squash courts, tennis courts, gym, sauna, Turkish steam bath, and massage.

Where to Stay

Pan Pacific ★★★★★
Jalan Putra
Tel: 60 (3)4425555
Fax: 60 (3)4417236

City center. Five hundred and forty-eight guest rooms and suites with recently upgraded Pacific (membership) floors. Fully equipped business center with laptop computer rentals.

Shangri-La Hotel ★★★★★
Jalan Sultan Ismail
Tel: 60 (3)2322388
Fax: 60 (3)2301514

Located in downtown Kuala Lumpur. Seven hundred and eighteen guest rooms and suites. Business center and doctor on call.

Ming Court Hotel ★★★★★
Jalan Ampung
Tel: 60 (3)2618888
Fax: 60 (3)2612393

Part of well-known Asian chain, located in downtown Kuala Lumpur. Business center with convention capabilities of up to 1,200 guests. Doctor on call, outdoor pool, sauna, and steam room.

Hotel Equatorial   Recommended****
Jalan Sultan Ismail
Tel: 60 (3)2617777
Fax: 60 (3)2619020

Located in the city center. Three hundred guest rooms and three restaurants. Business center and conference facilities, swimming pool. Older local hotel with good service, and value.

Park Royal Kuala Lumpur   Recommended****
Jalan Sultan Ismail
Tel: 60 (3)2425588
Fax: 60 (3)2415524

Three hundred and thirty-seven guest rooms and suites. Business center, doctor on call. Former Regent hotel.

Holiday Inn City Center   ****
Jalan Raja Laut
Tel: 60 (3)2939233
Fax: 60 (3)2939634

Situated in the city center. If you are going to this hotel by taxi, make sure you specify "city center" as there are two Holiday Inns in Kuala Lumpur. Business center, health center, pool, squash, massage services, doctor on call.

Plaza Hotel　　　　　　　　　Recommended***
Jalan Raja Laut
Tel: 60 (3)2982255
Fax: 60 (3)2920959

A less expensive hotel for the business traveler on a budget. For those who are planning to stay awhile, ask for their long-term rates. One hundred and sixty guest rooms, business center, and health center. Received the Malaysian Tourism Gold Award in 1988, 1989, and 1990 for excellence in hotel service.

Melia Kuala Lumpur　　　　　　　　　***
Jalan Imbi
Tel: 60 (3)2428333
Fax: 60 (3)2426623

Three hundred guest rooms and suites. Next to Imbi plaza, the computer mall.

Petaling Jaya Hilton
Jalan Barat
Tel: 60 (3)7559122
Fax: 60 (3)7553909

Three hundred and fifty-nine guest rooms and suites. Close to factory district. Mainly for the manufacturing businessperson.

Apartments
(For longer stays or with family)

Duta Vista Executive Suites *****
Persiaran Ledang (Just off Jalan Duta)
Tel: 60 (3)2552020
Fax: 60 (3)2550808

Closer to the city than MiCasa. Sixty-seven suites. Business center and personalized stationery. All hotel comforts and services (room service, housekeeping). Swimming pool, squash courts, in-house video. Each suite has two bedrooms, two bathrooms, a lounge, dining area, and kitchen. Luxury accommodation.

MiCasa Hotel Apartments ****
Jalan Tun Razak
Tel: 60 (3)2618833
Fax: 60 (3)2623979

Closer to Petaling Jaya than the city center. Two hundred and fifty suites, Mexican restaurant, and night life.

Airport Hotels

Merlin ***
Jalan Subang Jaya
Fax: 60 (3)7331299

One of an international chain located ten minutes from Subang International and 12 minutes from Petaling Jaya town center. One hundred and fifty rooms and suites. Business center, convention facilities with a variety of conference equipment, pool, health club, tennis courts, squash, golf, and gym. (See also Hyatt Saujana under the **Golfing Getaways**.)

Kuching Sarawak

Kuching Hilton ****
Tel: (82)248200
Fax: (82)428984

Fifteen minutes from Kuching International Airport, overlooking the Sarawak River. Business center, three hundred and twenty-two rooms, and three restaurants, swimming pool, gym, sauna, steam bath, tennis. Near Sarawak Golf Club. International chain.

Holiday Inn Kuching ****
Jalan Tunku Abdul Rahman
Tel: (82)423111
Fax: (82)426169

City center. Three hundred and twenty rooms, many restaurants, business center, pool, sauna, gym, steam, tennis, disco. Medical and dental help on call. International chain.

Riverside Majestic   **Recommended*******
Jalan Tuanku Abdul Rahman
Tel: 60 (82)247777
Fax: 60 (82)425858

Three hundred and eighteen rooms. More recreational facilities than Hilton and Holiday Inn. Business center.

Kota Kinabalu, Sabah

Hyatt Kinabalu International Recommended*****
Jalan Datuk Salleh Sulong
Tel: 60 (88)221234
Fax: 60 (88)225972

Located in Kota Kinabalu's business district overlooking the South China Sea, ten minutes from the airport. Three hundred and fifteen rooms and four restaurants, outdoor pool, business center. Near Sabah Golf and Country Club. International chain.

Shangri La ****
Bandaran Berjaya
Tel: 60 (88)212800
Fax: 60 (88)212078

One hundred and twenty-six rooms, business center, function rooms, health center, massage, gym, and sauna.

Golfing Getaways

Hyatt Saujana *****
Subang International Airport Highway
Tel: 60 (3)746-1188
Fax: 60 (3)746-2789

A resort for the serious golfer. Surrounded by two high-class golf courses in the Saujana Golf and Country Club. Two km (three mi.) from Subang International. Computerized business center and extensive conference and function facilities. Two swimming pools, sauna, steam bath, whirlpool, jogging track, and daily aerobics. International chain.

Awana Golf and Country Club *****
Genting Highlands

Located on the terraces of the Genting Highlands. Two heated pools, Jacuzzi, health center, and sports complex. Luxurious condominium-type accommodation. Located near Awana Golf and Country Club.

Park Plaza ****

Located 20 minutes from Malacca town, 90 minutes drive from Kuala Lumpur. Swimming pool, tennis, squash, table tennis, volleyball, horse and pony riding, three restaurants. Across from the 18-hole Ayer Keroh Golf Club.

Beach Getaways

Pangkor Islands

Pangkor Laut Resort   **Recommended****
Tel: 60 (5)291-375

Situated on a private 300-acre island, surrounded by virgin, two-million-year-old rainforest. One hundred and sixty-three villas; choice of beaches within walking distance. Resort in the jungle, over the water on stilts, and on the beach. Great views of the wildlife. Pool, squash, tennis, and a variety of water sports.

Note: Access to Pangkor Island by ferry from Lamut. We would gladly go back any day to enjoy the fabulous setting and Emerald Bay.

Pan Pacific Resort ****
Golden Sands
Tel: 60 (03)2913757

Conference center, water sports, 18-hole golf course, pool and tennis, 163 rooms, five restaurants and bars.

Langkawi

Langkawi can be reached by a short plane ride.

Pelangi Beach Resort *****
Tel: 60 (4)911001
Fax: 60 (4)911122

A member of the "Leading Hotels of the World." A tropical beach hotel.

Burah Bay Resort
Tel: 60 (4)911061
Fax: 60 (4)911172

A 400-room beach resort on a calm, white sandy beach. TV, air-conditioning, pool.

Datai Resort Recommended*****
Tel: 60 (3)2453515
Fax: 60 (3)2453540

Located on a 1,800-acre preserve of rainforest, 30 minutes from Langkawi Airport. Kerry Hill, an Australian architect, designed this resort keeping nature and the traditional kampong style in mind using marble, sandstone, and wood. Sixty-eight guest rooms and suites in a central building and 40 free-standing villas. Business center, 18-hole golf course, health club, beach club, mountain bikes available.

Island of Borneo

Sarawak

Rihga Royal Hotel Miri *****
Tel: 60 (85)421121
Fax: 60 (85)421099

This hotel sits on 20 acres of land on Brighton Beach, ten minutes from Miri International Airport. Two hundred and twenty-five rooms and a variety of restaurants, as well as a traditional English Pub, discotheque, and lounge featuring a string quartet. Business center and a theater-style function room which can hold up to 650. Outdoor pool, gym, massage rooms, and indoor spa pool. Billiards, darts, and backgammon are offered at the pub.

Holiday Inn Damai Beach   ****
Tel: 60 (8)2411777

Located 20 km (32 mi.) from Kuching, access by road or boat along the Sarawak River. Swimming pool, darts, table tennis, snooker, fitness center, sauna, whirl pool, 18-hole golf course, many water sports, bikes, nurse on call, convention rooms.

Royal Mulu Resort   Recommended*****
                                                (for the adventurous)

Tel: 60 (5)421121
Fax: 60 (5)421088

Sister hotel of the Rihga Royal Hotel, but not as classy and more for the adventurous. Situated on the Melinau River adjacent to Mulu National Park. Accessible by Malaysian Airlines through Miri or Limbang, the flight takes approximately 30 minutes and then five minutes by car or 20 minutes by boat. Those who are adventurous can take a seven-hour boat ride from Miri. Swimming pool, western food, air-conditioning, function room for up to 250. The resort has a mountain backdrop and a good view of Deer Cave where two million bats leave everyday at dusk. The entire resort is built on stilts three meters off the ground.

Where to Stay

Sabah

Sabandar Bay Resort ★★★★
Tuaran, Sabah
Tel: 60 (88)242884
Fax: 60 (88)242887

Located 40 km (64 mi.) from Kota Kinabalu; 45 minutes by car (optional hotel pickup). One hundred and six rooms, two restaurants, disco, business center, in-house movies, outdoor pool, scuba courses, and trips, canoeing, windsurfing, fishing, parasailing, bowling green, mini golf, and table tennis.

OTHER BUSINESS TITLES FROM SELF-COUNSEL PRESS

MALAYSIA: *A Kick Start Guide for Business Travelers*
by Guy and Victoria Brooks

Malaysia is a roaring Asian tiger with one of the world's most quickly developing economies. If you come armed with the right knowledge of how to do business, the rewards are well worth the effort.

This guide is for the business traveler who has little practical knowledge of Malaysia and the entrepreneur looking for new opportunities in Malaysia's high-performing economy.

The book tells you —

- how to get appointments with managing directors using proper business etiquette
- the best buys in Malaysian handicrafts
- the best spots to relax in if you want to combine your business trip with a vacation

Malaysia outlines in a concise, interesting, and often personal manner, the cultural idiosyncrasies that you need to know to be effective in business. The result will be an easier adjustment for you, which means your mind can focus on business matters, not on overcoming culture shock! $9.95

INDONESIA: *A Kick Start Guide for Business Travelers*
by Guy and Victoria Brooks

With an economic growth rate of over 8%, Indonesia is one of Asia's little dragons. It is predicted that by the next century, Indonesia will become a middle-income nation. The opportunities for foreign investment and expertise are boundless.

This guide is for the business traveler who has little practical knowledge of Indonesia and the entrepreneur looking for new opportunities in Indonesia's high-performing economy.

The book tells you —

- how to get appointments with managing directors using proper business etiquette

- the best way to get around

- where the new opportunities are for business

- the best spots to relax in if you want to combine your business trip with a vacation

Indonesia outlines in a concise, interesting, and often personal manner, the cultural idiosyncrasies that you need to know to be effective in business. The result will be an easier adjustment for you, which means your mind can focus on business matters, not on overcoming culture shock! $9.95

VIETNAM: *A Kick Start Guide for Business Travelers*
by Guy and Victoria Brooks

Until recently, Vietnam was closed to the outside world. Yet even before the U.S. embargo was lifted, businesses were clamoring to get a foothold in Asia's "Sleeping Tiger." Vietnam is still changing slowly, and anyone with patience and an eye for opportunity can get in now and be in for the long run. Markets and opportunities will grow for the next few decades as Vietnam comes of age.

The book tells you —

- how to get appointments with managing directors using proper business etiquette
- the best way to get around
- where the new opportunities are for business
- the best spots to relax in if you want to combine your business trip with a vacation

Vietnam outlines in a concise, interesting, and often personal manner, the cultural idiosyncrasies that you need to know to be effective in business. The result will be an easier adjustment for you, which means your mind can focus on business matters, not on overcoming culture shock! $9.95

BUSINESS ETIQUETTE
Make a good impression — gain the competitive edge
by Jacqueline Dunckel

Mind your manners and get ahead! Knowing when to open the door for a colleague or how to accept a gift can sometimes mean the difference between being pigeon-holed in your current position or being offered that attractive promotion. But times have also changed, and the rules once relied on are not always appropriate today. With the growing number of women in company boardrooms and the move toward more international business, a new style of behavior is often called for.

This book is as easy to pick up and use as a quick reference before that special event as it is to read cover to cover. $9.95

Contents include:

- Telephone manners
- Introductions and conversation
- Cultural courtesy
- Table manners
- Eating in and dining out
- Giving and receiving — the etiquette of business gifts
- Manners on the road

ORDER FORM

All prices are subject to change without notice. Books are available in book, department, and stationery stores. If you cannot buy the book through a store, please use this order form.
(Please print)

Name _____

Address _____

_____

Charge to: ❏ Visa   ❏ MasterCard

Account Number _____

Validation Date _____

Expiry Date _____

Signature _____

❏ **Check here for a free catalogue.**

IN CANADA
Please send your order to the nearest location:

Self-Counsel Press
1481 Charlotte Road
North Vancouver, B.C.
V7J 1H1

Self-Counsel Press
8-2283 Argentia Road
Mississauga, Ontario
L5N 5Z2

IN THE U.S.A.
Please send your order to:
Self-Counsel Press Inc.
1704 N. State Street
Bellingham, WA 98225

YES, please send me:

___ copies of **Malaysia: A Kick Start Guide for Business Travelers**, $9.95

___ copies of **Indonesia: A Kick Start Guide for Business Travelers**, $9.95

___ copies of **Vietnam: A Kick Start Guide for Business Travelers**, $9.95

___ copies of **Business Etiquette**, $9.95

Please add $3.00 for postage & handling.
Canadian residents, please add 7% GST to your order.
WA residents, please add 7.8% sales tax.

COMMENTS

Any comments you have on this or any other Self-Counsel publication are welcome. Please use space below.

_____
_____
_____
_____
_____
_____
_____
_____
_____
_____
_____